FINANCIAL CARE FOR YOUR ELDERLY RELATIVES

FINANCIAL CARE FOR YOUR ELDERLY RELATIVES

BEVERLY CHANDLER

LONGMAN

© Allied Dunbar Financial Services Ltd 1990

ISBN 0 85121-652-8

Published by
Longman Law, Tax and Finance
Longman Group UK Limited
21-27 Lamb's Conduit Street, London WC1N 3NJ

Associated Offices

Australia, Hong Kong, Malaysia, Singapore, USA

All rights reserved. No part of this publication may be reproduced, stored in a retrieval system, or transmitted, in any form or by any means, electronic, mechanical, photocopying, recording or otherwise, without either the prior written permission of the publishers, or a licence permitting restricted copying issued by the Copyright Licensing Agency Limited, 33-34 Alfred Place, London WC1E 7DP.

No responsibility for loss occasioned to any person acting or refraining from action as a result of the material in this publication can be accepted by the authors or publishers.

The views and opinions of Allied Dunbar may not necessarily coincide with some of the views and opinions expressed in this book which are solely those of the authors and no endorsement of them by Allied Dunbar should be inferred.

A CIP catalogue record for this book is available from the British Library.

The material herein which is Crown Copyright is reproduced with the permission of the Controller of Her Majesty's Stationery Office.

Printed and bound in Great Britain by Biddles of Guildford Ltd.

Every care has been taken in preparing this book. The guidance it contains is sound at the time of publication but it is not intended to be a substitute for skilled professional assistance except in the most straightforward situations.

Because of this, the author, the publishers and Allied Dunbar Financial Services Ltd (or any other company within the Allied Dunbar Group) can take no responsibility for the outcome of action taken or not taken as a result of reading this book.

Beverly Chandler

Beverly Chandler is a full-time freelance journalist who writes for a selection of newspapers and magazines on financial matters. Beverly spent two years working for the journal *Business* which involved running the popular *Portfolio* competition. She was also instrumental in setting up and running the *Financial Times* group's Offshore Adviser and has since specialised in offshore finance. Some examples of her work are financial guides to Jersey and to Guernsey.

Beverly lives in London and currently edits the newsletter, *Finance at 50 plus* and continues to contribute regularly to the *Financial Times, Money Magazine, Investment International, Portfolio International* and *European Investor* among others.

Preface

The elderly in this country are, in the main, sadly provided for. The State pension scheme and benefit schemes that were to be the mainstay of their retirement years are woefully inadequate. Unless carefully invested, the savings of the elderly will have been diminished by inflation.

It is increasingly likely that the responsibility for an ageing parent will fall upon you, their offspring, to ensure that they can maintain the quality of life they deserve until the end, and that means everyone needs to start planning now.

Contents

Preface vii

1 An ageing population 1
  Statistics 1
  Pensions 3

2 Basic State benefits 5
  The State pension 5
    Basic pension 6
    Graduated pension 6
    State Earnings Related Pension Scheme 7
    Widow's benefits 8
    The pension rules for divorced or
      separated claimants 9
    Claiming the State pension from abroad 10
    Claiming the State pension from hospital 10
  Other sources of financial help from the State 11
    The savings rules 11
    The rules on income 12
  Income support 12
    The pensioner premium 13
    The enhanced pensioner premium 13
    The higher pensioner premium 13
    Disability premium 13
    Severe disability premium 13
  Case studies 14
  Extra allowances 15
    Christmas bonus 15
    Housing benefit 15
    The social fund 15

x *Contents*

3 State benefits for the disabled or housebound — 18
Mobility allowance — 18
Invalidity benefit — 19
Attendance allowance — 20
Benefits available for carers — 21
Rate relief for the disabled — 21
The independent living fund — 21

4 State help at home — 22
Services available — 22
Overcoming disabilities — 23
Sources of finance for adaptations to the home — 24
   Home improvement grants — 25
   Intermediate grants — 25
   Repairs grants — 25
   Conventional loans — 25
   Interest only or maturity loans — 26
   Council grants — 26
Assistance with fuel bills — 27
   Meters — 27
Finance for health costs — 28
   Dental care — 28
   Opticians — 29
   Hearing aids — 29
   Prescriptions — 29
Cover for medical care abroad — 29
Help with legal costs — 30
Getting about — 30

5 Assistance provided by charities — 31
Major organisations — 31
Local charities — 33

6 Older people and housing — 35
Choosing a home — 35
Location — 36
Security — 37
   Alarm systems — 38
   Further tips — 38
Adaptability — 39
   Obtaining advice — 39
   Reputable builders — 40

Cost of maintenance	40
Tenants' responsibilities	41
Council or housing association tenants	42
Other schemes	42
Buying a property with limited capital	43
Leasehold schemes	44
Shared ownership	44
Loan stock or licence schemes	45
Discount schemes	45
Granny flats	46
Sheltered housing	46
Services	48
Selling the property	48
7 Caring for elderly relatives at home	**50**
The carer	50
The emotional implications	51
Questions to ask yourself	51
Help available in deciding	52
The financial implications	53
Extra expenses	53
Working restrictions	54
The physical implications	54
Basic nursing	55
Adapting your home	55
Where to get help	56
Practical help	57
Home visits	57
8 Residential care	**59**
How to choose a home	59
Grace Link	59
Elderly Accommodation Counsel	59
Counsel and Care for the Elderly	61
Residential care homes	61
Local authority homes	62
Paying for local authority residential care	64
Private residential homes	64
How to pay for private residential homes	66
Nursing homes	68
How to pay for nursing homes	69

9 Voluntary provision of residential homes — 71
Abbeyfield homes — 72
Distressed Gentlefolk's Aid Association — 73
Almshouses — 74

10 Medical and nursing care — 76
Nursing homes — 76
Care centres — 77
Private health insurance schemes — 77
Private nursing — 80
Medical care for the terminally ill — 80
    Hospices — 80
    Home units — 81

11 Legal aspects of illness — 83
Illness — 83
The living Will — 85
Consent to treatment — 85
Financial matters — 86
    Agents — 87
    Appointees — 87
Powers of attorney and the formation of trusts — 88
The Court of Protection — 89

12 Boosting income and capital — 91
Home Income Plans — 91
    Tax and the Home Income Plan — 92
Home Reversion Schemes — 93
Other possibilities — 94
    Interest-only loans — 95
    Investment bonds — 95
    Other points to bear in mind — 95

13 Your own pension arrangements — 96
Pensions — 96
    Occupational pension schemes — 97
    Additional Voluntary Contributions — 97
    Personal pensions — 98

14 Where there's a Will — 100
Making a Will — 100
Inheritance tax — 101

If there is no Will		103
How to be a personal representative		104
Deeds of variation		104
15 When someone dies		**106**
What to do		106
Registering the death		107
Medical aspects		109
Moving a body		109
What to do if someone dies abroad		110
Arranging a funeral		110
Paying for a funeral		112
16 Financial peace of mind		**114**
17 A final thought		**116**
Appendix: Useful addresses		117
Index		121

1 An ageing population

One of the leading human developments of the 20th century has been in our ability to control population growth. Through advances in our knowledge of medicine we have beaten many of the illnesses that wrought havoc on earlier generations. Through improvements in living conditions and nutrition, we have dramatically extended the human lifespan. At the other end of the scale, through the development of reliable forms of contraception, we have lowered population growth.

Statistics

The combination of these factors has caused major changes in the life expectancy statistics. The average life expectancy for women in the UK has gone from 52 at the turn of the century to 77 at its close. The picture is the same for men, who can now hope to live to an average of 71 years, easily beating the average 48 of 90 years ago. In 30 years' time the average lifespan for both sexes is predicted to be 77 (See graph on page 2).

If we take a look at the average age of the population in our country, this has gone from 34 years to 35 years in ten years and is projected to increase to 37 by the end of the century and to 40 in the first decade of the 21st century. By that time the average age of the UK's population will be closer to retirement than just starting work.

2 An ageing population

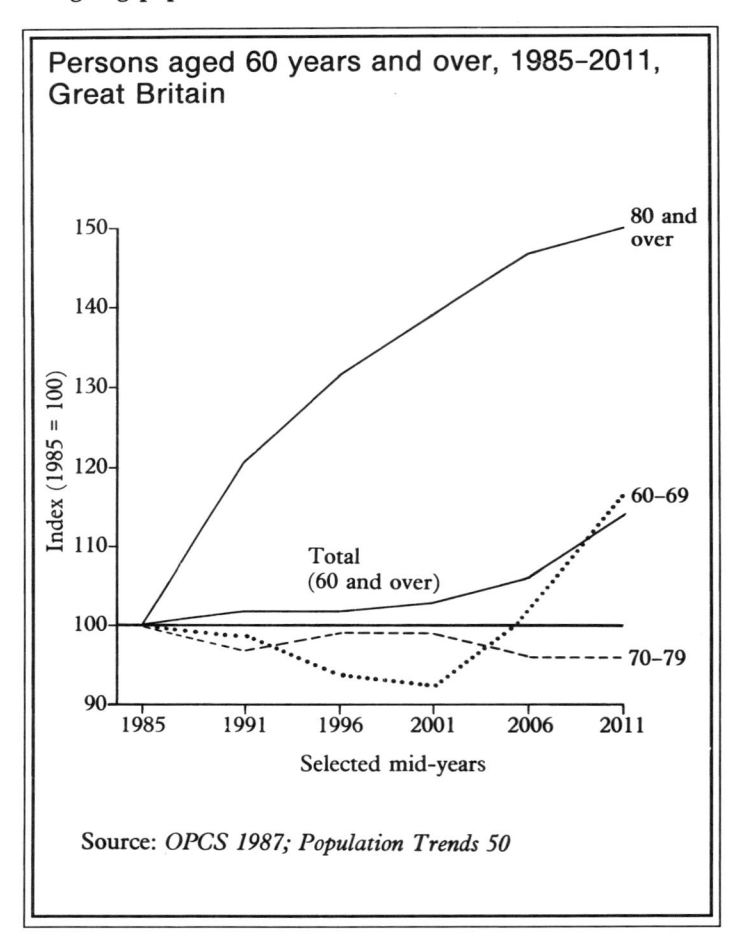

Persons aged 60 years and over, 1985–2011, Great Britain

[Chart: Index (1985 = 100) vs Selected mid-years (1985, 1991, 1996, 2001, 2006, 2011), showing four lines: "80 and over" rising to ~148; "Total (60 and over)" roughly flat near 100 rising to ~114; "60–69" dipping then rising to ~114; "70–79" slightly below 100.]

Source: *OPCS 1987; Population Trends 50*

The fact has to be faced that the UK, in common with the rest of Europe has an ageing population. One of the most significant causes is that we have a practically static population growth figure. Statistics show that since the 1970s, population growth has averaged roughly 0.1 per cent per year and projections show that we will only see a 0.2 per cent yearly growth in the size of the population up to the end of the century.

Pensions

So significant a change in what is a relatively short period of time has left those responsible for the financial well-being of the population, both in the State and the private sector, rather at a loss. The State has provided a pension to its retired population throughout the 20th century. The State pension is paid from the taxes and National Insurance contributions paid by the current workforce. This system worked very well while the balance was roughly equal and there were enough workers to pay for the retired. Nowadays, however, the balance has gone awry. Roughly one in five people in the UK are retired compared with one in 20 at the start of the century. That leaves roughly 11 million people in the retirement band. Only 1.5 million of these people are financially active.

At present the rate of 100 workers to 36 retired people means that the contributions from the remaining workforce are stretched to their limits to attempt to ensure that a State pension is a living wage. While there are many ways of coping with this problem, the UK Government has chosen to encourage self-reliance rather than State reliance to equip people for their old age. The Government is encouraging the workers of today to take out private, occupation-related pension schemes and is subsidising this move with tax breaks, worth an estimated £9 billion.

Unlike the State pension which is linked to prices, a job-related scheme may be linked to an individual's earnings. As earnings have increased faster than prices over recent years, an earnings related pension is likely to pay more money. Also, a private pension scheme is invested as a lump sum and the investment plan is designed to ensure that the cash keeps pace with the cost of living changes throughout the working life.

4 *An ageing population*

While the development of private pensions will ease the pressure of financing the current workforce when they get to retirement age, what about the 11 million people who are retired now and the legions more who will reach retirement in the next few years who remain dependent upon the limited resources of a State pension?

When Lloyd George introduced the pension in 1908 he gave retired men, who passed a 'moral fitness' test, roughly 20 per cent of the national average salary, the sum of five shillings. Today, at £43.60 a week the basic single person State pension is still around 20 per cent of the national average wage. At least today's pensioners don't have to prove their moral worth but they do have to live on an increasingly inadequate income. Statistics show that over 30 per cent of retired people are on the poverty line and over 50 per cent have disabling health problems. Further, the financial cost of care and support of an 80 year old is estimated to be five to ten times higher than that of a 60 year old. As the population gets older, it needs more money, not less.

With the State falling down on the job, reality shows that relatives are emerging as the main source of support, both financial and practical, for the elderly. Casting your mind back to the ever-expanding life expectancy figures, you are increasingly likely to find that you are gaining parents who are financially dependent on you. Both emotionally and practically you will need to be prepared. This book is intended to be a guide through the resources available to help you, as you yourself approach retirement and life on a fixed income, and to help your elderly dependants to continue to live an independent life but one that has the quality they deserve.

2 Basic State benefits

To assess the resources available for those who have retired, we need to start at the beginning, with a look at what the State provides. There is no quick and easy way to outline the State pension and benefits services. However, do not be put off, it is estimated that a significant proportion of elderly people are not claiming the benefits to which they are entitled. It is always worth checking whether someone is eligible for financial assistance if they are having problems making ends meet.

The older the retired person, the more likely it is that they are living on a basic State pension than an occupational scheme. While occupational pensions began to develop in the 1950s, until very recently the majority of the working population relied upon the State pension and individual investments to fund their retirement. Times are changing and it is likely that when the current workforce reaches retirement eight out of ten people will be in an occupational scheme.

The State pension

The State pension is made up of three parts and is payable once someone has reached the standard retirement age of 60 for a woman and 65 for a man.

6 *Basic State benefits*

Basic pension

The first part is the basic pension which is generally payable to anyone who has made National Insurance contributions for about 90 per cent of their working life.

Married women qualify for the basic pension either on their own National Insurance contributions or based on a husband's contributions, once he is receiving his pension and the wife herself is over 60 and effectively retired. If a wife is under 60 when her husband retires, her husband can claim for her as a dependant unless the wife earns more than £34.70 a week. Payment of the basic pension to a married woman is not dependent upon her living with her husband, once she has qualified for the pension it is hers for life.

For single people the basic pension amounts to a weekly £43.60. For married couples the pension is £69.80 a week. This figure represents roughly 25 per cent of national average earnings.

Earnings rule

In the 1989 Budget the government abolished the earnings rule for pensioners so that from 1 October 1989 a retired person could earn more than £75.00 a week without having their State pension reduced and they could work as many hours as they wished without being penalised. If a retired person does continue to work after retirement, they will receive their pension in full and are exempt from paying National Insurance contributions.

Graduated pension

The second part of the State pension is the graduated pension. This was introduced by the government in 1961 to supplement the basic pension and the scheme was in use until 1975. It was related to earnings, paying women 5p for every £9 in graduated contributions and paying men 5p for every £7.50, a maximum payment of £5.71 a week for every contribution. Normally this pension is paid with the basic pension but a retired person can receive the graduated pension even if they do not qualify for the basic pension.

State Earnings Related Pension Scheme

In 1978 the government introduced the third part of the basic pension, the State Earnings Related Pension Scheme, or SERPS as it is more commonly known. As SERPS is based on earnings over a 20 year period it is only fully effective for those who retire on or after 1998 so is unlikely to represent much of the pension that someone who has already retired receives.

For those who retire before the 1998 date SERPS pays out an additional pension which is earnings-related and based on the amount of earnings between the lower and upper earnings limits for National Insurance contributions in the complete years between April 1978 and the date of retirement. If there is any question of whether someone is receiving the right amount of SERPS pension, the DSS can do an assessment of contributions. Details of how to apply for this are available from the local social security office. Each part of the State pension can be claimed independently if circumstances allow and further details are available, again from the local social security office.

If someone remains in full-time work beyond the standard retirement age to 65, if a woman, or 70, if a man, the State pension is increased. The amount of increase that can be earned in the first year of deferring retirement is now 7.5p a week for every £1.00 of the pension for each year of cancelled retirement. If someone defers retirement for five years, the pension is increased by approximately 37 per cent.

The State pension can also be increased if the retired person has any other dependants, whether adults or children, as long as they are not in receipt of another benefit on their behalf.

8 Basic State benefits

There is a further pension available for people who were unable to work regularly during their life because of responsibilities at home, for instance looking after an elderly or disabled person or children. This is called the Home Responsibilities Protection scheme. It is awarded in respect of whole tax years from April 1978 during which the person was unable to work. Details on HRP are available from your local social security office.

A retired person who is over 80, is ordinarily resident in the UK and has no retirement pension qualifies for a non-contributory retirement pension of £26.20, as long as they have lived in the UK for at least ten years since their sixtieth birthday. An elderly person of 80 or over who does qualify for the full pension receives an extra 25p per week.

Widow's benefits

On 11 April 1988 the government changed the rules on widow's benefits. The widow's allowance was replaced by the widow's payment. Immediately a wife's husband dies, if she is under 60 and he has made the necessary National Insurance contributions, she will receive a single payment of £1,000 as a tax-free contributory benefit. If a wife is over 60 when her husband dies she will only receive the payment if the husband was under 65 and not receiving a State retirement pension. A divorced woman, or a woman living with another man as man and wife at the time of her husband's death does not qualify for this payment.

If the widow has dependent children, she will, subject to the same conditions, qualify for the widowed mother's allowance. In certain circumstances the widowed mother's allowance can be paid even if the child does not live with the mother. If she does not have children, she may qualify for the widow's pension. This is a regular payment which starts within a week of the death of the husband. Unlike the widow's payment, this is a taxable contributory benefit made up of a basic pension which is related to the wife's age when she was widowed or when her widowed mother's allowance ended plus a possible additional pension.

The changes in 1988 raised the lower age limit from 40 to 45 and raised the age at which the full-rate pension becomes payable from 50 to 55. However, those widows already receiving the widow's pension under the old scheme will continue to get it even if they are under 45.

To qualify for the widow's pension, the wife must have been 45 or over when the husband died. A claiming widow gets the full rate of pension if she was 55 or over when she was widowed and less if she was under 55. The top rate is £46.90.

In addition to the widow's pension, the widow may qualify for a proportion of the additional or graduated pension earned by her late husband. Once the widow herself reaches 60 she should qualify for the basic retirement pension plus half the husband's graduated pension.

The pension rules for divorced or separated claimants

If a retired person was either divorced or reached pension age after 6 April 1979 and cannot get a full pension based on their own contributions, they may be able to use their spouse's contribution record to increase their basic pension up to the maximum available of £43.60.

Women who were under 60 or men who were under 65 when they divorced can use their former spouse's contributions as their own either from the start of their working life or for the period over which the marriage lasted. This also applies in the case of retired people getting divorced after reaching retirement age. If either spouse remarries before retirement then they have no claim on the former spouse's contributions but if they remarry in retirement the original entitlement still stands.

Women who separate from their husbands during retirement but do not qualify for a pension on their own contribution records can claim the married women's pension of £28.20 but only after the husband has claimed his pension.

Claiming the State pension from abroad

It is becoming increasingly popular for the elderly to spend the winter months away from the UK, seeking the better weather in southern Europe for example. If an elderly person does plan to go away for the winter or even longer, they need to do some planning ahead in order to continue to receive their pension.

State pension orders cannot be cashed more than three months after the date printed on them, so collecting a pension while abroad depends on how long the retired person is planning to stay away. If it is under three months they can save all the orders up and bank them on their return. For trips of over three months the retired person can arrange with their local security office to pay the pension into a UK bank. If the trip overseas is likely to be for a substantial amount of time, it can be arranged for the pension to be received in the country being visited. However, unless it is a country within the European Community (EC) any increase in the pension may not be paid.

Details on claiming the State pension abroad are available from your local social security office or the DSS, Overseas Branch. (See Appendix).

Claiming the State pension from hospital

If a retired person is unfortunate enough to have to go into hospital for any length of time it can affect their pension. For the first six weeks they can receive their pension as usual, however, on the basis of receiving free treatment, after that the pension is usually reduced. If they have a dependant the pension will be reduced to £8.70 a week and if they are on their own, a reduction to £17.40. If they are hospitalised for one year the pension goes down to £8.70 a week.

Other sources of financial help from the State

In addition to the basic pension, there are a variety of other schemes designed to help bring a retired person's income up to the basic level set by the government.

The major source of additional income for the older person without significant private savings is income support. Up until 1988 this was called supplementary benefit and was, in many cases, higher than the new income support.

A retired couple are eligible for income support as long as their savings are not over £8,000, they have a low income and neither of them work for more than 24 hours a week. Under the rules for income support, men and women are considered a couple when they live together.

The savings rules

The £8,000 savings limit applies to couples, in which case their savings are added together, or single people. Savings of less than £3,000 do not affect somebody's eligibility for income support. However, if a retired person has savings of between £3,000 and £8,000 the State considers this an income of £1.00 a week for every £250 (or part of) over £3,000. If somebody tries to cut down their savings by spending them or giving them to their family they may well find that the State still considers they have the savings. If such a decision is made, the elderly person can appeal.

12 Basic State benefits

All the usual forms of savings are counted under this scheme, such as cash, bank accounts or equity investments. If the person has joint savings with someone who is not retired, then half of those savings are considered to be theirs. The only savings which the State will ignore are the capital value in a privately owned house, the eventual surrender value of a life assurance policy and any amounts of State aid which are still owed for up to a year.

The rules on income

Income is considered to include any payments from an occupational pensions scheme, the State pension scheme, or any other benefits. For couples the amount is added together.

There are some forms of income which can be ignored under these requirements. Benefits such as housing benefit, which is explained further on in this chapter, attendance allowance, mobility allowance and interest or dividends from savings under the £8,000 limit are exempt. Also, the first £5.00 received from a war widow's pension, a war disablement pension or any regular payments from relatives or friends is exempt. If the retired person has a lodger in their house then the first £4.00 of rent is exempt and if that lodger pays rent which includes an extra charge for heating, the first £11.00 is ignored.

Income support

The rate of income support is £34.90 for a single person or £54.80 for a couple a week. In addition to that there are five premiums which can be included for the elderly or disabled.

The pensioner premium

This applies to those who are single and aged between 60 and 79. In the case of a couple, both must be under 80 and one of them must be over 60. The amount payable under this premium is £11.20 for a single person or £17.05 for a couple.

The enhanced pensioner premium

This is available to those aged between 75 and 79. A couple are eligible for this premium when they are both under 80 but one of them is over 75. This premium is worth £13.70 for a single person or £20.55 for a couple.

The higher pension premium

This is available for those aged 80 or more or those aged between 60 and 79 who receive an attendance allowance, invalidity benefit, severe disablement allowance, are registered blind or are provided with an invalid carriage. In the case of a couple only one person needs to fulfill the conditions. The amount available is £16.20 for a single person or £23.00 for a couple.

Disability premium

This is an extra payment for those under 60 who are disabled and also qualify for other disability benefits such as the mobility allowance or attendance allowance. The rates are £13.70 for a single person or £19.50 for a couple. Only one partner needs to qualify in the case of a couple.

Severe disability premium

This is the only premium that can be paid in addition to the others. In order to qualify, the retired person needs to be

14 *Basic State benefits*

living alone and receiving an attendance allowance. Confusingly, there are exceptions to the living alone condition. Someone may still qualify if they are living with another person who receives the attendance allowance or someone who is acting as a carer, although this will affect the amount of payment available. Under the severe disability premium, a single person or a couple where only one partner qualifies would get £28.20 while a couple who both qualify would get £56.40. The various extra payments available for the disabled or housebound elderly person are more fully outlined in Chapter 3.

If a person's income or pension plus any of the above premiums amounts to less than the low income stated, then the difference becomes eligible as income support. Calculating whether someone is eligible for income support and how much that might be, requires some simple mathematics.

Case studies

Mr and Mrs Brown are aged 71 and 72 and live in a housing association flat. They have joint savings of £2,500 and their only income is the State pension assessed on Mr Brown's contributions only. Their income is £75.10 a week from the State pension. Their personal allowance as a couple is £57.60 plus the pensioner premium of £17.95 for couples, a total of £75.55. This means that they are eligible for the difference between the two sums, an extra 45p a week.

Mrs Smith is 71 and lives on her own in a council flat. She has savings of £550. Her only income is her State pension of £46.90. She is eligible for the pensioner premium of £11.80 plus her personal allowance of £36.70, a total of £48.50. Her actual income is £1.60 less than that so she would qualify for income support for that amount.

Extra allowances

There is further help for retired people who own their own homes. The Department of Social Security will make extra allowance for those facing mortgage interest, ground rent, some service charges or, if savings are under £500, the interest on a home improvement loan.

Christmas bonus

Anyone who is in receipt of a retirement pension; attendance or invalid care allowance; over 80s or widow's pension; invalidity pension, income support after pension age or war widow's or war disablement pension and is living in the UK or the EC during the first week of December qualifies for the Christmas bonus. This is a tax free amount of £10.00 and is usually paid automatically to those eligible and has no effect on other benefits.

Housing benefit

This is a benefit which is organised by the local authorities under instruction from the government. It is payable to those who have difficulties maintaining payment on their homes, either with rent or community charge.

From April 1990 the rates system operating presently in England and Wales has been replaced by the Community Charge or poll tax, as it is more commonly known. The poll tax was introduced in Scotland in April 1989. Under the poll tax system, rebates will be handled in much the same way as under the previous rates system.

Housing benefit is available to those with a low income, whatever their age, who have less than £16,000 in savings and have a commitment to pay rent or rates. Those who own their own home and are on a restricted income can apply for

16 *Basic State benefits*

a rate rebate but under this benefit no help is available for mortgage repayments or other charges connected with owning a house.

Housing benefit can pay out as much as 100 per cent rebate on rent, including service charges and up to 80 per cent rebate on community charge bills. Service charges included in the sum for rent rebates include such facilities as an emergency alarm system in sheltered housing for the elderly or disabled, the cost of a warden or the cost of cleaning if the tenant cannot manage this themselves.

The calculations used to assess whether someone qualifies for housing benefit, are much the same as for income benefit, outlined earlier. The potential applicants need to work out their savings, and their income and then compare it with their personal allowance. If their income is less than the personal allowance, they should get help with rent and community charge. However in the case of rent rebate, no reduction can be made for heating costs if they are included in the rent and the amount payable is affected if the claimant has a lodger.

The payment of housing benefit is not affected by the claimant going away for a period of up to one year, unless they sublet their house, in which case it is not payable. If, in the opinion of the local authorities, someone is claiming housing benefit for an unreasonably high rent, they may not be eligible. However there is a contingency fund under which the authorities can pay the benefit to someone they consider to be in a dire financial state. Full details of the housing benefit are available from the local social security office.

The social fund

This is designed to make lump sum payments either as loans or outright payment for those with a low income and suffering a sudden crisis or exceptional expense. Normally they are only available to those on income or housing benefit, although application for a crisis loan is available to anyone in an emergency.

The social fund will pay the costs of a basic funeral, for instance, depending on the savings and income of the person organising that funeral. Help is also available for those on income support faced with the cost of moving, upkeep on a house or emergency travel. Those on income support and aged over 60 can get £5 a week towards fuel costs if the average temperature is zero degrees centigrade or below for seven consecutive days.

3 State benefits for the disabled or housebound

The last chapter outlined the basic pension or benefits available to anyone who has retired. In this chapter we will investigate what is available for the elderly person who has the specific problems of disability or immobility. For the retired person who is either unable to get around much or needs a lot of care and medical attention there are a variety of extra allowances that the State provides to help with the cost of those services. Details on all of the benefits given below are available from the local social security office.

Mobility allowance

The mobility allowance is designed to help the disabled or housebound get out and about more. It is available to people who are classified as disabled, or have been, since before retirement. In order to qualify, the claimant needs to have become unable or virtually unable to walk before reaching 65. The physical condition must be unchanged for at least one year and claimants must have been living in this country for at least 12 of the last 18 months.

Someone who is eligible for the mobility allowance must make a claim before their 66th birthday. Once granted, payment can continue until they reach 80 years of age.

The weekly rate of the mobility allowance is £24.40 and it

does not depend on National Insurance contributions, is not affected by the amount of savings or income the claimant has and in turn it doesn't affect any other pension or benefit they receive. Also it can be paid to claimants wherever they live, in a hospital or an institution or at home.

As the main aim of the allowance is to encourage mobility for disabled people there are also some concessions on car usage connected with the allowance. If the claimant has a car or someone else, maybe a friend or relative, uses their car almost exclusively to drive the disabled person around, that car will be exempt from road tax.

The car-owning claimant should also be eligible for the orange badge scheme which allows parking in some restricted areas. These badges are issued by the local authorities and in some cases there is a small charge.

Invalidity benefit

While this mainly applies to those who are under pension age and unable to work through ill-health, those who are claiming it can continue to claim beyond the normal pension age. That means that women up to 65 and men up to 70 can continue to claim the invalidity pension of £43.60 for a single person, £26.20 for a dependent adult or £8.95 for a dependent child.

Depending on the age at which someone became unable to work or the amount of earnings since 1978, they may be eligible for the invalidity allowance as well. The weekly rates of this allowance are £9.20 for those under 40, £6.20 for 40-49 and £3.10 for men aged between 50 and 59 and women aged between 50 an 54. For the retired person there is an advantage in continuing to receive invalidity benefit because it is not taxable, unlike the State pension.

Attendance allowance

The attendance allowance is available for people who are severely disabled, whether mentally or physically. Like the mobility allowance, the attendance allowance is not dependent on a history of National Insurance contributions, it is not taxable, nor is it affected by savings or income and does not usually affect any other benefits the claimant receives.

There is no upper age limit for this allowance. To qualify the claimant must have lived in the UK for a minimum of 26 weeks of the last 12 months and must have needed the care of another person for at least six months.

The allowance is split into a higher or lower rate. The higher rate is available for those who need help both during the night and the day and the lower rate is for those who need daytime or night-time care only. The amount is £37.55 for the higher rate and £25.05 for the lower rate. If the claimant's medical condition becomes so severe that they are hospitalised or have to go into a home, the allowance is stopped after four weeks. However, if the claimant is in hospital paying for all the hospital services as a private patient or in a private home or hospice, they can continue to receive the attendance allowance.

Unfortunately it is inevitable that in order to prove that someone needs enough care to qualify for the allowance they will have to undergo a medical examination. If it seems likely that an elderly person qualifies for the attendance allowance they must not be put off by the formality or apparent intrusion of the application process. If it seems that the eventual amount awarded is not correct, then it is possible to appeal.

Benefits available for carers

If someone has given up work and is unable to return because of giving full-time care to a severely disabled person, whether or not they are a relative, they may qualify for the invalid care allowance. To be eligible the carer must be over 16 but under pension age when they first claim. Also the carer must spend at least 35 hours a week looking after someone who is receiving an attendance allowance.

The Independent Living Fund

Established in 1988 this is a special fund aimed at helping the severely disabled to remain relatively independent of institutional care. To qualify, the applicant has to have savings of less than £6,000, and a low income, live alone and need extensive help from others, both personally and domestically. Details of this fund are available from the Independent Living Fund.

The benefits listed above are available as a source of added income for the day-to-day living costs of a disabled or housebound person. In the next chapter, we will look at the local grants and services available for elderly people.

4 State help at home

The previous chapters have outlined the sources of money available from the State to help with day-to-day living costs for the elderly or disabled person. However, if someone's need is more specific, perhaps an adaptation or repair to their house or a regular home-help to aid with domestic routine, there are services available throughout the country, supplied either by local government or by local charities. In this chapter we will explore the services provided for the elderly by local authorities.

Modern thinking on care for the elderly is slanted towards attempting to provide someone with a greater degree of independence than has been possible in the past and for as long as is practical. This means that there has been a growth in the number of services available to help fulfil that aim.

Services available

Many elderly people would prefer the independence and quality of life available through living in their own home. Of course, ensuring that this is possible means that one should look after one's health and generally keep fit and active throughout one's life. However, even someone who has become quite frail or suffers with their health can manage at home given the right resources.

Unfortunately the level of services available for the elderly varies widely around the country. Also, the recent cutbacks in local government budgeting has meant that often there are not enough staff or resources available for our ageing population, so it can be frustrating when attempting to find out about local schemes. It is worth persevering however as just that little bit more help at home can make all the difference.

The first port of call in attempting to find out what is available and how someone might be eligible is the local social services department. This can be contacted directly, or more information might be available through a GP, health visitor or a social worker.

Most areas will run the basic schemes of a regular home help or meals on wheels service, although the quality and the cost of these services vary from place to place. Some areas have extensive day care facilities, where the elderly person either goes to a centre for the day or has a carer with them in their homes. Other schemes which might be available include lunch clubs, a sitting service to give carers a break, nailcutting, chiropody, a mobile library or even gardening or decorating services.

Overcoming disabilities

If the elderly person has a specific medical problem, regular care can be obtained through the GP and a team of district nurses and health visitors. This might include after-hospital care or physiotherapy. In some cases, the district health authority can provide night nursing facilities or nursing services for particular areas of ill health, such as for those who have suffered a stroke or suffer from incontinence. For someone who has a particular disability, but is not necessarily registered disabled and needs an adaptation or alteration to their home in order to increase mobility and remain relatively independent, most local social services departments have occupational therapists who can advise on changes and help with applications for funding in order to carry out the work.

As with most areas of local authority work, there are not enough occupational therapists available, so waiting for an appointment can be frustrating. However, again it is worth persevering. Once they have visited and made an assessment of someone's needs, the occupational therapist can advise on local architects or surveyors who specialise in designing for disabled people. In some areas there are schemes known as agency services which give specialist advice on adapting a disabled person's home. Under the scheme, advice is given throughout the project on plans, estimates, surveys, grants available and approvals required. Details on whether such a scheme operates locally should be available through the local Citizens' Advice Bureau or the council's housing department.

Anyone considering building work to their home should get all the professional advice possible and use companies that belong to a reputable trade organisation.

Sources of finance for adaptations to the home

If someone is considering building an extension or altering their house to enable them to continue living there throughout old age, there are various options open to them on the financing of those changes. Firstly, they can obviously use their own savings. While that might be the quicker option because of the inevitable delay involved in getting State help, it is worth investigating the options available from the local authority.

Home improvement grants

The home improvement grant is a discretionary award granted by the local council to people with mobility problems who need an adaptation such as the installation of wheelchair ramps or lifts or the moving of a bathroom to the ground floor. Except in the case of a disabled person, these grants are usually only given on properties built before 1961 and with a maximum rateable value of £400 in Greater London or £225 elsewhere. Scotland has a different system again, so check with the local authority's housing department for exact details.

Intermediate grants

Intermediate grants cover the installation of basic facilities into a house, such as plumbing for hot and cold water and an inside lavatory. There should be no problem with obtaining one of these grants if someone doesn't have these basic facilities.

Repairs grants

These are discretionary again and are usually only available towards the cost of major structural repairs, rather than any routine maintenance, on an older property built before 1919.

Conventional loans

For the homeowners who wish to make adaptations to their homes, some building societies and banks will make small loans to cover the cost. If the homeowners have a mortgage which they have virtually paid off, it is worth keeping a tiny amount of the mortgage in operation in order to maintain their position as existing borrowers. They should then get priority when seeking further funding and can rest assured that the deeds to their house are in safe-keeping with the lender.

Someone considering taking out a loan to cover the cost of building work should be quite certain that they can afford to repay that loan, even if interest rates go up. Because the borrower may be paying off capital and interest, repayments can be quite high. Obviously anyone seeking a loan should be very wary of independent lending agencies as many are run by the unscrupulous and charge interest at prohibitive rates or quote deceptive rates.

Interest only or maturity loans

Some local councils and some building societies offer loans to the elderly on which the borrower only pays the interest. The capital is repaid when the house is finally sold. This is one option for elderly people with a limited income and whose only capital is locked up inside their house, but they need to be fully aware that they are borrowing against their only asset, their home.

Council grants

If the adaptations to the house are relatively minor, for instance the installation of a safety rail next to the bath, or light fittings at a convenient height, some local councils will supply these aids. Similarly, some councils will fund the fitting of an alarm system to a flat or house, either connected to a local control centre or operating as an independent system. The contribution the elderly user will have to make for this varies from borough to borough, so contact the local council or apply for a visit from an occupational therapist for more details.

Elderly people who receive income support or housing benefit can apply for grants to cover the cost of fitting insulation or draughtproofing to their houses. Eligibility for the insulation grant is lost if they have started fitting insulation before applying for a grant or if they already have insulation of roughly one inch in thickness. The draughtproofing grant is only available in areas where the scheme is run, but for those on income support or housing benefit it can pay for up to 90 per cent of the cost of the materials. To find out whether such a scheme is running locally, contact Neighbourhood Energy Action (see Appendix).

Assistance with fuel bills

Fuel bills are often the major expense for someone who is living on a limited income. If a problem does develop with payment of bills from the Electricity Board or British Gas, the user must contact the relevant company immediately. Under their Code of Practice, neither service should cut off a household between 1 October and 31 March which has an occupant living on a pension but this does not apply if there are clearly enough funds to pay the bills.

Funds to cover extra heavy bills for pensioners during particularly harsh winters are available from the social fund as outlined in Chapter 2. Some people find it easier to budget for fuel bills through fuel stamps which can be bought at some post offices or the electricity and gas showrooms. The stamps can be used for either gas or electricity. Another solution may be to make regular payments all through the year with the overpayment during the summer compensating for the underpayment during the winter.

Meters

To be entirely certain how much heating and light are costing, the installation of a slot meter may be a solution. If someone is living in privately rented accommodation and using a slot meter, they should check that they are paying the correct rate, and not paying extra to keep their landlord in his retirement. Information is available from the fuel boards. Some people find a budget meter a good solution. These are installed by some fuel boards and are operated by a token or key, allowing the user to be certain of how much fuel they are using. In some instances a loan or grant from the social fund may be available to cover the cost of installing a meter, however there is no installation charge for the budget meter.

Finance for health costs

The 1989 Budget introduced tax relief on eligible private medical insurance for the over 60s, including tax relief for someone who funds a medical insurance policy for someone over 60 to receive the tax relief. This will come into effect on 6 April 1990. However, if an elderly person's resources don't stretch to private health care, there are various grants available under the NHS to help towards those costs that are not covered by the public health scheme.

Dental care

It is not always clear when someone visits the dentist whether they are being treated as a private or NHS patient. It is a good rule always to establish this first. Those patients who are receiving income support qualify for free dental treatment, including the fitting of dentures and regular check-ups. This also applies to those who are in hospital. Those who are not on income support but have a low income and less than £8,000 in savings also qualify for reduced fees. The dentist should have the relevant forms or contact the social security office for further clarification. If an elderly person is not eligible for a discount on dental treatment because of their income, they only have to pay up to the first £150 in dental fees.

Opticians

Since April 1989, opticians have been allowed to charge for a standard sight test. However, those who are on income support or belong to certain high risk groups, such as the registered blind, the partially sighted or those who suffer from glaucoma, and their immediate family, are eligible for free eye-testing. This also applies to some people with a low income. People in the same low income group who need glasses can get a voucher either to cover the cost of a NHS pair or to be put towards a new more expensive pair.

Hearing aids

Hearing aids are usually prescribed after examination by the GP and testing of hearing at a local hospital. A prescribed NHS hearing aid and its batteries will be supplied and fitted free.

Prescriptions

For women aged over 60 and men aged over 65, prescriptions are free. Furthermore, surgical supports, such as elastic stockings, are free to hospital outpatients within the same age limits and outpatients on income support also qualify for free fabric supports and wigs. Inpatients also qualify for these.

Cover for medical care abroad

It is a popular misconception that visitors to the EC are entitled to free medical care while abroad. The system is not standardised and some may discover too late that they have to find the money to pay for treatment themselves.

If someone elderly is planning to go overseas, they should check with the local social security office whether they are covered for medical treatment in that country. If not, then it is advisable to get medical insurance for the duration of the stay. Unfortunately, it is wise to bear in mind the cost of flying someone back in the event of death on holiday. This can be prohibitively expensive so check that this kind of eventuality is covered by travel or medical insurance.

Help with legal costs

The amount of low cost legal advice available for those on a fixed budget varies from one solicitor's practice to another. Retired people with limited means needing legal advice, should first visit the local Citizens Advice Bureau. The bureau will be able to recommend local firms of solicitors who offer a free initial half hour interview with a solicitor or else ones that charge a maximum fee of £5 plus VAT for that period. Those who are claiming income support or have a low income may qualify for free or heavily subsidised legal advice and assistance. Should it be necessary to go to court then Legal Aid is available for those who meet the financial requirements.

Getting about

Anyone living in the UK and aged 60 or over qualifies for the Senior Citizen's Railcard allowing discounted fares on the British Rail network. There is also a European version which allows retired people to receive discounted fares around Europe. For those who are registered disabled there is a Disabled Person's Railcard which covers the holder and companion, allowing discount travel. Travel on local tube or bus networks might also be discounted for retired people. This varies around the country so investigate further at a local station or travel centre. Some airlines and travel firms offer concessions to the retired. Details of these schemes should be available from your local travel agent.

5 Assistance provided by charities

We are very fortunate in the UK in having a tradition of charitable giving, both in terms of money, but perhaps more importantly, also in terms of time and commitment to good causes. With the current climate of cutbacks of State services for those in our society who have limited means or particular needs, the charitable provision of help is becoming increasingly important.

Major organisations

Many of the local authority schemes outlined in the previous chapter are now likely to be run by well-trained and professional volunteers, often drawn from the ranks of the fellow-elderly. The best way to find out what charitable assistance is available for the elderly around the country, is to approach one or more of the voluntary organisations themselves. The three major organisations working specifically for elderly people are Age Concern, Help the Aged and the Centre for Policy on Ageing. These three agencies work together with the common aim of changing attitudes towards older people and protecting their needs, whether in housing or health.

Age Concern, formerly the National Old People's Welfare Council, is the largest charity operating in the field. Founded in 1940, Age Concern now has 1,400 independent local

Assistance provided by charities

groups operating in the UK, with 130,000 volunteers running local schemes providing services to elderly people. The local Age Concern branch is likely to run anything from a lunch club to an Over-60s club, plus offer practical advice on any problems elderly people are likely to come up against.

Help the Aged concentrates its efforts on raising money to support a wide range of activities both in the UK and overseas. With the aid of a Help the Aged grant many local volunteer groups have access to minibuses to help the immobile get out and about or can install the Lifeline system, an emergency communications system for the elderly. Help the Aged also runs a scheme whereby older people can donate their house to the charity and hand over the responsibility for all maintenance, rates and insurance to Help the Aged. In return the homeowners can continue to live there for as long as they wish.

The Centre for Policy on Ageing is a centre for academic and practical study of the needs of older people. The CPA publishes a wide variety of booklets on aspects of care for the elderly and actively supports the University of the Third Age, the university for the retired.

Contacting any of these agencies is a step to achieving a better quality of life for an elderly person, particularly someone in poor health or worried about money. Other organisations that provide services for the elderly include the WRVS, which often runs a local meals on wheels or visiting service for elderly and relatively housebound people. Another agency worth contacting is the British Red Cross Society which in some areas can help with advice and volunteers for simple nursing care for older people.

Local charities

Some local groups run 'good neighbour' schemes for the elderly who live on their own. This means that a volunteer can regularly visit an older person, at a convenient time, and help around the house with a specific need or just have a cup of tea and a chat.

Older people living in rural or isolated areas have a problem with mobility, particularly since some local bus services have been scaled down. Many local voluntary agencies have raised money and volunteers run either a minibus service or a car-sharing scheme, where those who have a car offer lifts to others.

Many of the local voluntary organisations can help with the less serious, but still very important, problems of being elderly and housebound. For instance, some areas have hairdressers who can come to an older person's house and do their hair, others have a theatre-group made up of older people who do performances at hospitals or retirement homes.

Age Concern, Preston has a novel scheme for small repairs or renovation of furniture. An elderly person who needs a piece of furniture repaired or renovated can leave it with Age Concern. For just the cost of the materials, a local team of disabled workers will repair it. Local volunteer agencies will often work with each other for a particular aim. The Peace of Mind scheme, run in Gateshead last year, saw over 1,500 elderly people's homes being fitted with security devices and the scheme was extended to include those housed by the local council. Staff provided by the Manpower Services Commission are running a Crime Prevention and Energy Advice Centre on behalf of Age Concern, Avon. They give advice on security or energy queries but can also fit simple security devices, such as bolts and chains as well as install insulation and draughtproofing. Contact addresses and phone numbers for all the organisations mentioned above are listed in the Appendix.

6 Older people and housing

They say that home is where the heart is and for elderly people this becomes even more important as they are likely to spend more and more time in their homes as they get older. Planning ahead is an area where the 'young retired', concerned for their own retirement or for the elderly in their family, can be particularly useful.

Choosing a home

The best time to start considering housing options for retirement years is *before* retirement. Hopefully at that point there is the money and the energy to plan ahead and be objective about future needs. However, life is full of uncertainty and often the best laid plans are ruined by a change in circumstances, so ideally a certain flexibility should be included in long-term plans.

Many elderly people remain fit and active for the rest of their lives and are quite capable of living on their own with the minimum of help from friends and relatives. However even if health is not specifically a problem, everyone finds that as one gets older, a lack of agility and energy can make even the most simple tasks quite a burden. Forward planning and use of the wide variety of aids available can help ensure that independence is not threatened and that the quality of life can be maintained during retirement years. Location, security, adaptability, and cost of maintenance are the main points to consider when assessing a home for the retirement years.

Location

Location is extremely important. Is the older person living close to relatives or friends who could help out in an emergency? What are the local transport services like? Even if the elderly person drives a car, they should bear in mind they might not always be so mobile. Is there a hospital or health centre reasonably close by? What are the local shops like? Is there a convenient post office or bank for cashing cheques? Do the local social services department or local voluntary organisations run schemes in that area?

If the attraction of the area relies on proximity to relatives, are they likely to move? Is the area changing, becoming more urban or more rural for instance, and how will that affect those living there?

Also bear in mind interests and hobbies. If the older person is a particularly keen walker or church goer, they deserve the option of living within easy travelling distance of places where they can enjoy their interests. Similarly around the home itself, keen gardeners can get a lot of enjoyment and, incidentally, exercise, out of keeping a garden. However, gardening is a strenuous activity and if the garden is too big, it can become a burden.

These days councils are trying not to house elderly people at the top of skyscraper blocks of flats where, though the views might be extensive, they can get stranded by a broken lift for as long as it takes the lift to be repaired. However, it is still not unheard of for elderly people to live in high-rises. Although they will get priority on applications to move, waiting lists are notoriously long, so planning ahead becomes all the more important.

When considering the location of a house for retirement years, do not forget aesthetics. If someone is spending more time at home, views out of the windows and the amount of light and sunlight in the rooms become more important. Changing the location by moving house is the biggest and most expensive option for an elderly person, whatever their resources, and not one to be undertaken lightly. It is worth spending plenty of time discussing it with relatives and friends and being as objective as possible in making a decision.

Security

This covers personal security from burglary as well as safety in the home from domestic accidents. In these times it is all too common to hear of elderly people being burgled for even the most paltry sums of money. Most houses can be made more safe by fairly simple adaptations and fittings, so if the house is ideal in location, moving need only be an option in extreme cases.

Local police stations have a crime prevention officer who can advise on security arrangements for a house. A CPO will visit anyone's home, analyse what security devices are needed and recommend inexpensive locks and bolts that can really help in deterring burglars and allow the older person to sleep more easily at night.

In many areas the local authorities or charitable organisations arrange schemes for installing simple security devices, only charging for the cost of the parts. Furthermore, this is an area where members of the family can help out, installing window locks, door chains or viewers in the front door. Something as simple as adequate lighting around the outside of a house can keep a burglar away and lessen the chances of someone being mugged on their way into their house.

Alarm systems

Alarm systems connected to a control centre or to the homes of other members of the family can be extremely comforting for the elderly. In some areas the local authorities are now offering these to their tenants and to others, for a rental fee which can sometimes be paid by the social services, as outlined in Chapter 4.

Most systems work through the telephone network. Pressing a button on a pendant or activating the alarm through a panic button in the house means that the elderly person is immediately in contact with a control centre, or by telephone to their family or close friends. The ideal sort of alarm allows two-way speech so that the exact nature of the problem can immediately be diagnosed and help summoned. It is also possible to get a system that dials a list of relatives or friends in turn and automatically switches itself back on if no-one can be contacted. For more specific details of alarm systems available contact the local Citizen's Advice Bureau (*CAB*), Age Concern office, or the public library for the *Which?* Consumer Guide which has a report on personal alarm systems.

Telephones themselves can be an essential means of communication in a crisis. An elderly person should avoid having a wall-mounted phone in case they fall and cannot reach up to the telephone and summon help.

Further tips

The adverse side of too much security in a home is that it can affect personal safety. When installing security devices for someone elderly, every care should be taken that that person can get out in a hurry if they need to, for instance if there is a fire. Also a friendly neighbour or local member of the family should have a spare set of keys to the house, so that in an emergency someone could get in and offer help. Personal safety can be further ensured by checking such things as wiring and plumbing in older houses. Stairs and bathrooms can also be accident prone areas. Fitting a handrail to the stairs or a rail to help someone get out of the bath can make these simple activities much safer. The bath itself can have non-slip strips fixed on the inside and stairs need bright lighting and non-slip carpeting.

Adaptability

If an older person is extremely happy in their house but not coping well with its existing layout, it might be possible to adapt it to allow greater mobility. This can stretch from quite simple changes as outlined above, such as fitting safety rails, to major rebuilding or extensions. Adaptations that might make life easier for an older person include installing a bathroom or bedroom on the ground floor or putting ramps up to the house's entrances. If the idea of transferring living arrangements to the ground floor seems to be the only solution to any problems developing, remember that a closed-up top floor will become damp and may lead to a significant loss of heat unless it is aired and properly looked after.

Obtaining advice

The funding possibilities for adaptations and building work were outlined in the previous chapters. Remember that if anyone living in the house is disabled then the local authorities are required to help them with housing adaptations. If someone is considering extensive building work under one of the schemes organised by the council, they should be given contact names for specialist advice and help with seeing the project through its various phases.

40 *Older people and housing*

If the person is on their own and needs advice on possible adaptations, a call to the CAB or local Age Concern group might prove useful. Some local housing associations or voluntary organisations have surveyors or architects who can occasionally advise elderly members of the general public for a fixed fee or sometimes, under the Chartered Surveyors Voluntary Service, although this is not available in all areas.

Reputable builders

Choosing a builder is something which requires some care as there are plenty of tales of woe. The best solution is to rely on personal testimonials from friends who have had building work done or try asking a local housing association or the council's housing department. Obtain at least three estimates from three different builders before making a decision. A useful source of information on builders is the National Housebuilding Council (see Appendix). Also try and choose builders who are members of either the Building Employers Confederation or the Federation of Master Builders. Where builders are members of these two organisations, the consumer can pay an extra one per cent of the cost of the work and obtain a guarantee that the work will be fully completed as agreed and if any problems develop later, these will be fixed by another builder who is a member of the organisation.

Cost of maintenance

The cost of maintenance of a house is an important part of the equation when the elderly are considering the feasibility of staying in a present house over the advantages of moving. House maintenance is one of those problems that gets bigger if left alone, rather than going away. From the roof to the foundations, things can be steadily breaking down without anyone noticing until it's too late and very expensive.

The solution is to do a thorough survey of the house when considering whether to stay there or move. If it is in relatively good order and likely to stay that way through sensible up-keep, there is unlikely to be a problem. If it is possible financially, it is always a good idea when doing any home maintenance to spend the money on quality materials and have any jobs done professionally, as they arise, rather than suffer in the long run. For those with limited financial resources there are grants available from the local authorities for the installation of draughtproofing and insulation in order to cut down on fuel bills. These were outlined in Chapter 4.

Tenants' responsibilities

For elderly tenants of council or housing association properties, the worry about major external repairs is not their responsibility. Everything to do with the plumbing or the wiring and the external structure and decoration of the property is the responsibility of the council or the association.

Internal decoration is usually the responsibility of the tenant, but some councils or associations run a decorating scheme for the elderly and as long as there is no younger person living in the property, an elderly person may qualify.

Under the 'Right to Repair' scheme, council tenants can do repairs costing between £20 and £200 on their flats themselves and claim all or part of the money back from the council. This is an extremely complicated system so seek advice about it first.

Elderly private tenants can face the worst battle of all in making landlords make repairs to their houses, particularly if they are sitting tenants. If the usual routes in trying to get repairs done have been exhausted all tenants have the right to call on the local authority's environmental health department to inspect the problem and even pursue the matter to the courts.

If, once all these considerations have been taken into account, it still seems that the best solution is to move house, there are a wide set of options available in terms of housing for the older person who is still relatively fit and active.

Council or housing association tenants

The relatively fit council or housing association tenants who wish simply to move somewhere more convenient or closer to their relatives should first visit their housing department or association's office. Because of the shortage of public sector housing, many councils and associations require their tenants to have lived within their area for a certain length of time before they can apply to move. Some of the larger housing associations will consider a move to another area if it can be proved that the applicant has strong personal ties to that area, for instance it is where all their family live. Council house tenants can expect a better response from another council if they are nominated as in need of moving by their own council. Ironically, their own council will only nominate them if they are on the top of a waiting list or classified as urgently needing to move and many tenants have never gone on their own council's waiting list because they wanted to move out of the area.

Other schemes

Another option might be the National Mobility Scheme, introduced by the government to help people who wish to move out of their present area. Most of the councils belong to this but few donate many vacancies to the scheme. A further option is the Tenants' Exchange Scheme which allows any tenant to swap his property with another tenant's. It is operable throughout Great Britain but only to or from Northern Ireland.

There is a private scheme also available to council or housing association tenants. For a fee of £15.00 or £10.00 for those on low incomes, the Locatex Bureau (see Appendix) will attempt to match tenants wishing to move from area to area. They handle enquiries for between 1,500 and 2,000 people at any one time.

For housing association tenants who live within a 100 mile radius of London there is a further scheme to help those who wish to move. Known as the Housing Associations' Liaison Office, they can nominate tenants from one association to another. But be warned, the waiting lists for housing association property can be very long. Details on this and other queries on housing associations are available from a regional Housing Corporation office.

The 'Right to Buy' scheme brought in by the government during recent years to enable council tenants to buy their properties, presents an alternative for the elderly person. Generally the requirement is that someone has been a council tenant for at least two years. The properties concerned are sold at a discount, often substantial, which can make the option appear very attractive. Details are available in the Government booklet 'Your right to buy your home'. However, purchasing the property will undoubtedly affect any benefits that person currently claims and means that they are now responsible for the upkeep of not only a mortgage but also insurance, maintenance and a service charge. If the property is then sold within three years, a proportion of the discount the ex-tenant receives must be repaid to the council.

Buying a property with limited capital

The schemes outlined below can be a useful alternative for ensuring adequate housing for an older person with a limited amount of capital. They can also be used for an older relative, in that the younger members of the family may be able to raise the capital on behalf of the older person, while occupation and actual ownership is restricted to that older person. However, all these schemes need careful consideration. Anyone considering them should get professional independent advice from someone who is familiar with the laws on the taxation of the elderly and families in general.

Leasehold schemes

These schemes are usually run by housing associations and usually apply to sheltered accommodation. This is accommodation that has been specially designed for the independent and fit and active elderly person. It is usually low-level, has a full-time warden, built-in security and personal alarm systems and has maintenance staff to look after the buildings.

Under the leasehold scheme, the potential resident buys say, a 70 per cent share of the lease and ultimately receives back 70 per cent of the value on selling. The remainder of the lease is paid for by government subsidy. The problem with these schemes is that the owner is then responsible for service charges, which cover the cost of the warden and the maintenance staff plus fuel bills and water rates. Someone considering this option should be quite certain that they have sufficient income to meet all these responsibilities. Further details on the leasehold schemes are available from the local Housing Corporation office.

Shared ownership

This is proving a useful option for council tenants who wish to buy their council properties. Usually offered by housing associations or councils and occasionally by building societies, the shared ownership scheme involves part-buying and part-renting of property. The older person buys as much of the lease as they can afford and pays rent on the rest. Usually, they are allowed to increase the amount they own when they are able, perhaps on the maturity of an insurance policy for instance. Further details on the shared ownership schemes are available from the local Housing Corporation office.

Loan-stock or licence schemes

Under these schemes, usually run by housing trusts or property developers, the older person makes an interest-free loan to the management company in return for which they get housing, often sheltered housing and the right to live there for life. The loan is repaid when they move but there is no interest paid on it. The amount of capital required for these schemes varies as do the terms of repayment. For instance, some schemes only repay the money once the property has someone living in it again and even then make deductions for the cost of organising that. Anyone considering one of these schemes should take reliable legal advice before making a commitment.

Discount schemes

Some developers of sheltered housing for the private market offer discounts on the properties. The terms of such deals vary substantially. In some cases the older person pays up to 75 per cent of the asking price and gets back the same proportion of the value of the property when they finally sell. Under other schemes though, all the buyer will ever get back will be the amount that they put in, despite the value of the house. Under some new schemes the entire value of the property goes back to the developers when the owner dies, so they have effectively only bought a lifetime's interest in that property. The size of the discounts offered depend on whether the applicant is male or female and is computed in terms of life expectancies. An older man living on his own will be offered a larger discount than a younger retired woman, for instance. These schemes need to be studied very carefully and independent legal and financial advice must be sought.

Granny flats

This popular term covers all sorts of accommodation which is basically attached or close to the older person's family unit. It is still not very common in this country, perhaps largely because of the cost of building or converting an existing space. The idea is that the elderly relative lives with the family but is self-contained and can maintain some degree of independence without being too far from help in an emergency.

Deciding whether this is a good option for you and your family is a very personal decision. Things to bear in mind when considering this option include the financial side, will your elderly relative pay rent and will that affect their benefits? On a more personal level, how will both sides of the family cope with each other in terms of maintaining privacy and coping with the differing lifestyles of people of different ages?

Sheltered housing

As mentioned in an earlier chapter, modern thinking on care for the elderly is that maintaining independence for as long as possible can mean a better quality of life for older people. This can often be made easier if there is a supply of houses or flats specifically designed to be suitable for the needs of an elderly person but allowing them to remain practically independent. As a result sheltered housing, offering many of the resources the elderly need, has seen something of a boom.

Older people and housing

It is possible to get sheltered housing through both the public and private sectors. Councils now have some sheltered housing, called extra-care sheltered housing, which offers a slightly higher degree of care than is normally available with sheltered accommodation, for instance some offer a meals service. As is to be expected this sort of housing is not widely available in the public sector and waiting lists tend to be long.

If someone can afford to consider the private sector, they will find that there is a bewildering amount of sheltered accommodation on offer and careful research needs to be done to ensure that they obtain a property that is truly a home and has no financial or legal strings attached. An excellent book which aims to help older people through the sheltered housing maze is available called the *Buyer's Guide to Sheltered Housing* from Age Concern.

Apart from the major concerns of whether or not the older person can find something they actually would like to live in situated in a suitable location, the key points to watch out for in looking at sheltered housing schemes are the purchase price, the service charge, the facilities provided and what happens if, due to ill-health, the purchaser becomes too frail to cope on their own.

The potential purchaser of a sheltered flat or house should expect to pay the normal market value of the property and buy it, in England and Wales at least, on a long lease. If they are being offered the property at a discount they should look carefully at the lease and the conditions of the repayment of capital value, as outlined above. Someone living in sheltered accommodation will meet their own fuel bills, community charge etc, so these need to be taken into account when calculating the amount of income needed to live there.

Services

For the supply of the very facilities that make it a sheltered property, the potential purchasers can expect to pay an annual service charge. This covers the cost of a warden, who is only there to check maintenance on the building, help in a crisis and keep a neighbourly eye on residents, fuel bills for the common parts of the scheme, building insurance, the cost of maintenance to the external structure of the property and the garden and the management organisation's administrative expenses. A ground rent may also be charged, the cost of which and how much it can be increased should be outlined in the lease.

Facilities provided in sheltered housing complexes vary considerably but there should be at least the services outlined above plus in some cases a guest room for residents' visitors, a communal laundry and maybe a communal room for occasional get-togethers.

Selling the property

If someone living in sheltered accommodation becomes more frail, they are still entitled to the local authority and voluntary services outlined in the previous chapters. They can still have meals on wheels or a home-help to aid in domestic routine. If someone becomes too frail to continue on their own, most leases allow the management organisation of a sheltered housing scheme to advise or even move somebody on to more full-time care. It is unlikely that this would actually be enforced and the idea is to protect other residents from disturbance, not to make someone less secure in their own home. However, if the time has come to sell the property and move on to a greater degree of care, the management organisation will normally control the sale to ensure that the property goes to another elderly person.

If sheltered housing does seem a viable option, look for established companies that have perfected the art of designing, building and running sheltered schemes. From April 1990 there is a code of conduct for builders and providers of sheltered housing. If they do not abide by the code they face possible expulsion from the National House-Building Council's register. Details of the code are available from Age Concern. When buying sheltered housing, always seek reliable independent legal advice and ensure that there will always be sufficient income to cover the regular cost of service charges plus the regular outgoings on domestic bills. Employing a few simple safeguards can make sheltered housing a pleasant option for older people.

7 Caring for elderly relatives at home

In the last chapter we dealt with the choice of housing for elderly people and how existing accommodation can be adapted to fit the requirements of someone who is becoming more frail. If continuing to live in their own home is no longer possible, the next set of options includes the possibility of looking after an elderly relative in your home and accepting the responsibility of caring for them permanently.

The carer

It is estimated that over six million people in the UK provide long hours of care for someone, usually a relative, who is elderly or disabled. You might not think of yourself as a carer, but if you have an elderly relative living with you who needs full-time company, personal help and supervision, you are a carer for that person. The greatest number of carers come from the age range 45 to 64 years old and 50 per cent of carers look after someone aged 75 or over. Until recently, carers were largely ignored. Those who took an elderly person back into the close family unit had little in the way of support, either financial or on a day-to-day basis. Since then the carer's task is an easier one. There is now a social security benefit, the invalid care allowance described in Chapter 3 and the new £10 a week payment starting in October 1990 — aimed at helping with the costs of caring for someone at home. There is also a growing band of support groups and organisations set up to help support the carer. These are discussed in more depth at the end of this chapter.

Making the decision to take a dependent person into your home and provide them with full-time care is extremely difficult. The decision needs to be seen in terms of the emotional, financial and physical implications. It would be much worse for both you and the dependent relative to discover too late that for any of these reasons the situation is not going to work.

The emotional implications

If your elderly relative has become so frail that the doctors and social workers are recommending they go into hospital or a residential home and they are not happy with that option, you will naturally want to help. Your emotional reaction may also be mixed with a sense of duty. Maybe your own children have just left home and there is plenty of room for a new addition to the household. Maybe you have worked in a caring profession, such as nursing, and feel that you can offer the best care to your elderly relative.

Questions to ask yourself

Whatever your instinctive reasoning, you need to stop for a while and look at the wider picture. Imagine that the emotional pressure is not there and try and assess the situation as you would if anyone else suggested coming to live with you and your family. Do you and your relative have a happy relationship? This might sound like an obvious question, but it is extremely relevant. You might have a good relationship with someone you see once a week or talk to on the telephone, but will that relationship stretch to having that person there, in your home, 24 hours a day?

In the case of a parent/offspring relationship, at least you are likely to have the advantage of knowing what it was like to live together. It might be a long time ago, but think back, did you get on well as a family then? On what sort of subjects did you clash and are they subjects that are still likely to cause a problem? These can stretch from the banal differences of opinion such as which television programmes you watch, up to the controversial issues of religion or morals. Do you like each other now? Are you able to talk and joke together? Do you still share interests? The closest people can become irritated with each other under stress, and trying to keep your life and their lives going can be extremely stressful.

If you are contemplating taking your parent into your home to live with your family, you need to think about the whole family's relationship with that person. How will it affect the relationship with your spouse and your children? Will you feel guilty for devoting some of your time to your parent rather than them? Would you count yourself as an independent person who enjoys being able to get out and about? Will you be able to accept the inevitable loss of liberty?

Much depends on how your relative feels about living with you. Are they choosing that option because of fear of the other choices, living in a residential care home or nursing home, for instance. You both need to sit down and examine all the choices for their future.

Help available in deciding

The exercise of drawing up a list of fors and againsts can be very useful in making a decision. If you do this with your relative, you will get a clearer idea of what they want from the future and arriving at a decision together could bring you closer together.

Caring for elderly relatives at home 53

While you are contemplating becoming a carer, do some research in your neighbourhood on what support groups or facilities are available for those in your position. The amount of help for carers varies from region to region but even if you only meet with one other person in your situation, it will be a relief to know that you are not on your own. Details on how to contact caring groups are listed in the Appendix.

The financial implications

The financial implications of living with an older person are not just the obvious 'one more mouth to feed'. Old people need more resources and money, and as they get older their needs increase. A rising grocery bill is likely to be the least of your worries.

Extra expenses

The cost of special aids to help mobility in the house; taxis or the use of a car to help with mobility out of the house; higher fuel costs because of the need for more heat in the home; the cost of nursing help or 'sitters' to allow you the occasional evening off, all these things need to be considered when making that decision.

If you are receiving some form of supplementary benefit, the payment will change if you combine households. It might not always change for the better, for instance if one of you has savings over £8,000, this could weigh down against you or your relative in calculating benefit. You will need to sit down and analyse your incomings and outgoings with an extra person in your household and without. You can get advice on benefits from your local social security office or a local voluntary agency such as the Citizens' Advice Bureau or Age Concern office. More specific private financial planning advice is contained in Chapters 12 and 13 of this book. There you will find details of various financial schemes you can subscribe to, which will ensure that, even when you retire, there will be enough money to cover the needs of your dependent elderly relative.

Working restrictions

If you are working, and plan to continue, but maybe change to part-time work in order to devote time to your new household, you will need to discuss the implications of that with your employer. Caring for someone who is frail is not a job that can be restricted easily to fit in with certain hours. How will your employer feel if some days you are late for work or have to take leave at short notice? Continuing to work may be your emotional release and essential to your being able to continue with caring at home, so you will not wish to jeopardise your job. Discuss your problems with your employer or your personnel officer and find out if any of your colleagues are in a similar situation. Just finding that you are not alone can make the problems seem more manageable and maybe you could arrange a flexible job-share with a fellow carer.

The Rochdale Carer's Charter is a recent addition to the field of support for carers. The ageing population statistics we discussed in Chapter 1 are affecting employment trends as well. As the number of available employees goes down, many companies are becoming more flexible about employing staff with other commitments. The Rochdale Carer's Charter is aimed at employers and outlines ways that staff who are also carers can be helped to fulfil all of their responsibilities. It is available from the Carers National Association (see Appendix).

The physical implications

Much depends on how much physical care your relative needs now and will need in the future. If you are not used to nursing someone you will need to ask yourself some questions. According to statistics released by the King's Fund Centre's Informal Caring Programme, roughly 50 per cent of carers over 45 are suffering from a long-standing illness themselves. This can be caused by a mixture of the physical and emotional strain of caring for someone for long hours.

Basic nursing

Physically, you need to be strong enough to support or lift an elderly person out of bed, up or down the stairs, in or out of the bath, to the lavatory or just actively looking after them. Emotionally, can you cope with worry or lack of sleep? Elderly people generally sleep less, and mentally confused people can sleep very little and need constant surveillance. Will this cause you enormous problems? Are you squeamish? Will problems such as incontinency or changing dressings overwhelm you? The older person needs to think about this too. Will the lack of dignity in being dependent on their own child for the most personal of tasks upset them? There are resources, such as a district nurse or nursing auxiliaries, who can help provide skilled nursing but you will almost certainly find that at some point you will need to do some basic nursing yourself for an elderly relative.

Adapting your home

Physical implications can also cover where you live. Take a good look around your home. Is it suitable for an older person who might develop mobility problems? Is it safe for someone who is mentally confused? Is the location convenient for hospitals, doctors, shops, good neighbours or other forms of help? Could it be adapted to provide a suitable environment and what would that be likely to cost? If you do consider moving in with an elderly relative at their house or both of you moving to something more convenient, you should get good advice on the financial and legal implications of doing this.

Whatever you decide once you have considered all these questions and arrived at an answer, you will need support. If you have decided that the role of carer is not for you, you are likely to feel guilty. However, the point of the whole exercise is to ensure a good quality of life for your elderly relative. Moving them in with you and finding that it does not work could be more traumatic and more seriously affect your relationship with them, than the initial blow of refusing their request.

If you do decide to become a carer, it can be very rewarding both for you and your relative. There is a wide range of support groups and resources available to try and make it easier and more rewarding for you both.

Where to get help

The first step is with the social services, either through your GP or a social worker or both. Many of the resources outlined in earlier chapters in this book will still be available to an elderly person, even though they are living with you. For instance, you may find that they are entitled to a home help, meals on wheels or a care attendant as detailed in Chapter 3. In some areas you may have low priority on waiting lists for these forms of support. The assumption may be that a woman can cope better than a man. If you suspect that this is the case, continue to ask the social security department for help. You will need all the help that you are entitled to if you are providing full-time care for someone who is physically or mentally frail. Do not forget that these services are paid for out of taxpayers' money and are there for taxpayers to use.

Practical help

Through the social services department you can also find out about day care centres or Alzheimer's Disease centres which could give you a day's rest a week or look after your relative while you are working. If your relative needs more specific care there are a variety of other resources available. District nurses can help you with regular nursing tasks that are required and may be able to help you get the additional aids or services for your relative. These may include help with incontinency problems, gadgetry to help with lifting an elderly person or special mattresses or beds to help with bedsores or mobility problems. Occupational therapists, covered more fully in Chapter 3, can give advice on practical problems and arrange or organise the supply of benefits or facilities for specific cases.

Home visits

For those who care for someone who is mentally confused, suffering from dementia or other mental health problems, some district health authorities have community psychiatric nurses who can visit your home and check on the health of a patient and their carer. This can be very comforting for a carer who has little experience of mental health problems and can find them disturbing and unpredictable.

Some local authorities, health authorities or voluntary agencies now run care attendant schemes. The extent of these varies from area to area, but the idea is to supply help where it is needed to people who care for others. Care attendants are usually quite flexible in when they visit and in what they do. If you need specific help with bathing an elderly person, or just time off to be on your own or go shopping, a care attendant can help. You can find out if there is a local scheme through the Association of Crossroads Care Attendant Schemes (see Appendix). Another source of information for carers is the Carers National Association and what was formerly called the National Council for Carers and

58 Caring for elderly relatives at home

their Elderly Dependents (see Appendix). This organisation can tell you if there is a local support group near you and advise you on other organisations that can provide help. You can also try the local branch of the Council for Voluntary Services, listed in the phone book. Do not be discouraged if there is no local group set up for carers. Contact the King's Fund Centre's Informal Caring Support Unit (see Appendix). This organisation is a source of information, education and training for carers and the professionals who work with them. They can supply you with leaflets on how to set up a local support group and reading lists of useful publications on the subject. A useful book recently published on behalf of the Health Education Authority and the King's Fund Centre is *Caring at Home* by Nancy Kohner. It costs £2.50 and contains all the information a potential or actual carer would need.

8 Residential care

In the previous chapter we outlined the pros and cons of caring for elderly relatives in your own home, both in terms of their happiness and comfort and your own. As we said, caring is a full-time job and the good carer is one who knows when to say enough is enough and admit that he or she does not have the resources to keep going. This chapter will look at residential homes, what level of care they can provide, how much they are likely to cost and how they can be paid for.

The longer someone lives, the more likely it is that they will become frail. Over 20 per cent of people aged over 80 suffer some sort of loss of mental acuity; 10 per cent of people aged over 85 have problems getting in and out of bed on their own. The statistics tell the tale and it is a fact that we will all have to face that living to an extreme age can mean that we become more dependent on outside help. If this happens the most caring thing that can be done for all concerned will be to call in professional help. The best sources for advice on the options at this point are the doctor or a social worker, from the local social services department. These professionals will assess someone's needs, ideally involving the elderly person's family as well, and are likely to recommend a residential home or hospitalisation, in extreme cases.

Moving into residential accommodation for the elderly can be a very traumatic step for that person and their family. Unfortunately the image of residential care is of a complete loss of independence and a subjection to very regimented routines. Inevitably for a caring family there will be guilt-feelings of having failed in continuing to care for the older person and providing them with the quality of life they deserve, right up to the end. It does not have to be like that. There is a wide variety of residential homes and the availability of options is not totally bound by the availability of finance.

How to choose a home

For those elderly who are offered a place in a local authority residential care home, there is likely to be little choice in places on offer, as explained below. However, if the elderly can afford to look at the private sector there are a variety of sources of information about private residential or nursing homes. The first source of information is likely to be the social security office which will have a wide range of information on local homes in all the sectors. Beyond that, there are the usual sources of information for elderly people, the Citizens' Advice Bureau and the local Age Concern group, which will have reading lists of books with relevant information. There are also some charitable organisations that have extensive nationwide lists of places.

Grace Link

This is a nationwide service listing the accommodation available in private residential or nursing homes. The service works from a database which is updated after annual visits to the homes included. There is a charge of £23 for the initial search but any further searches are free.

Elderly Accommodation Counsel

That is not a misprint. This charitable body describes itself as something one can talk with, rather than sit on. It has a vast database which covers all forms of residential accommodation available to the elderly. They do not give specific recommendations but can produce a list of places operating area by area and within a price range set by the enquirer. The service costs £5 or is free for those on a low income. Details from Elderly Accommodation Counsel (see Appendix).

Counsel and Care for the Elderly

This organisation can give advice on charitable grants available to help the elderly plus it is a source of some charitable funding itself. It also has a lot of information on voluntary residential accommodation around the country. Counsel and Care for the Elderly is open weekdays except Wednesday during office hours (see Appendix).

There are three types of residential care home, each representing the three sectors, state, private and voluntary. In this chapter we will examine the state and private sectors while the voluntary or charity run homes are looked at in the following chapter.

Residential homes are divided into two types and confusingly they are regulated by different authorities. The home that is designed for someone who has basic care needs but does not need special nursing is a retirement care home and is regulated by the local authority. A nursing home, where more special skills are provided, is authorised by the District Health Authority. There are also a few homes that offer all levels of care and are authorised by both authorities.

Residential care homes

The residential care home which is specifically run for older people appears under a variety of titles. However, whatever its name the principle is the same. It is a home for elderly people who need help with the personal day-to-day tasks of washing or going to the lavatory but do not need specific nursing attention.

All residential homes for the elderly, whoever runs them, are authorised by the local authority, the council. Under the Registered Homes Act 1984 all residential care homes with more than four residents must be registered by the local authority. The 1984 Act was brought in after extensive scandal and appalling tales of mismanagement had all but wrecked the image of residential homes. Prior to the Act, anyone with enough space in their house could take in elderly people, without having any checks on their suitability as providers of care to the elderly. At £1, the registration fee payable was too low to fund any regular checks on how that home was run. The 1984 Act requires registration of a home, dictates the number of residents a home may look after, controls the quality of staff for the home and requires regular inspections to ensure that it is conforming to set standards of care, hygiene and facilities. The 1984 Act was further supported by a voluntary code of practice for home-managers, Home Life, produced on behalf of the government by the Centre for Policy on Ageing.

Home Life sets out the level of care and the protection of rights that can be expected in a home. A copy is available from the Centre for Policy on Ageing but bear in mind that, unlike the Act itself, this is a voluntary code of practice and not enforceable by law. However, a good guide to a well-run home is whether it employs the Home Life code of practice.

Local authority homes

The establishment of these in England and Wales dates back to the National Assistance Act 1948, which required local authorities to provide residential accommodation for local people on low incomes who needed care because of frailty or

Residential care 63

disability. In England and Wales the part of the Act that refers to the provision of residential homes is Part III, so if a social worker starts referring to accommodation under Part III, that is what they mean. In Scotland, the foundation of local authority homes is controlled by Part IV of the Social Work (Scotland) Act 1968.

Local authority homes vary considerably around the country. They can be purpose built or converted from older houses, spacious or cramped. Council-run homes tend to be larger in terms of the number of residents than those in the private sector and it is not unheard of for someone to have to share a room. These homes are usually run by people trained in the social services and the variety of facilities available varies from home to home.

The Registered Homes Act 1984 does not apply to local authority homes, in terms of regular inspections of their premises. This means that there is often a significant disparity between the conditions of a local authority home and a privately registered home in the same borough. One is inspected and required constantly to maintain the standards required under the Act and the other is not. Applying for a place in a local authority home can be a lengthy procedure. The number of places available rarely matches up with the amount of people who need them so the waiting lists can be long and the choice limited. Usually, someone will only be offered a place in their local authority's catchment area, so going into a home near relatives in another area may be tricky.

Even though there is little choice of places available in council-run residential homes, everyone has the right to inspect the accommodation offered thoroughly and spend a short time staying there for a trial period. If someone is still very unhappy with the home, they can apply for a relocation but, again, this can take a long time.

Paying for local authority residential care

Priority for places in these homes is usually given to those who have low incomes and are in the greatest need. By law, local authorities have to do a full assessment of someone's finances before calculating what they should pay towards the cost of their care. In the case of a couple, where one spouse needs residential care and the other remains independent, the financial assessment is done on both their finances and a spouse might be required to help support the other one if there is enough income to do so.

The national minimum charge for a local authority residential home is £34.90 a week, but rates above that vary from local authority to local authority. So if someone receives the basic retirement pension of £46.90 they will pay the minimum charge of £36.70 a week and have £8.70 personal spending money left over. In this instance any short-fall between the minimum charge and the actual cost is paid for by the local authority. If someone has an income lower than the basic retirement pension and has savings of under £8,000 they qualify for income support to make up the difference, as outlined in Chapter 2. Someone with income above the basic retirement pension will pay more than the minimum charge and how much they pay is scaled up to a maximum figure above which the local authority will make up the difference.

Private residential homes

The end of the seventies and the opening years of the eighties saw a boom in the number of privately run residential homes for the elderly. This was because many in the private sector saw a gap in the market between the number of elderly people needing residential care and the number of places available in local authority homes. Because there is a greater level of choice about moving into a private rest home, the standard has generally been quite high. A home could not afford to get a reputation for being badly run as its intake of residents would fall. However, the passing of the 1984 Act ensured that standards were reasonably consistent and hopefully closed the few appallingly run private homes that dominated the headlines.

A privately run retirement home with more than four residents must be registered with the local authority and the certificate of registration must be displayed somewhere prominent so that visitors can see it. A further sign of a well-run home is membership of either one of three organisations formed to ensure that residential homes, whether nursing or rest, maintain high standards. These organisations are the British Federation of Care-Home Proprietors, the Registered Nursing Home Association and the National Confederation of Registered Rest Homes Associations. Each organisation has a symbol. These are pictured below, and seeing one of these signs should mean that the home is well-run.

NCHA

British Federation of Care-Home Proprietors

MEMBER

REGISTERED NURSING HOME ASSOCIATION

The charges for private residential homes vary widely and it is a golden rule not to expect that the more money charged, the better the facilities and care. What makes a home a pleasant place to live in varies as much as what someone wants from it. While some elderly people would like to retain as much independence as possible, others may want a variety of communal activities and so on. The only way to tell whether it is suitable is to visit, chat with other residents and to spend time talking with the staff. Often the entire atmosphere of a private home is dictated by the manner of the manager. On a purely personal level the elderly person should meet the manager and decide whether this is someone who is like-minded on what a home should provide for elderly people and is a kind and caring person.

How to pay for private residential homes

As outlined earlier, the cost of a private residential home can vary enormously, from maybe £200 a week to £300 or £400. For someone who has few financial resources, the cost of private care can initially appear well beyond their means. However, because there is a shortage of local authority residential care places, the Department of Social Security is forced to rely on the private sector and will help out with the cost. To qualify for help with fees for private residential homes, an elderly person needs to fall within the guidelines for income support as set out in Chapter 2. Beyond that, the Government has set national limits on how much it will pay per week in income support for the various forms of residential care and the various forms of disability or age of claimants.

As at 1 November 1989 the maximum weekly rates for income support towards the cost of private residential care are:

Maximum weekly rates

	£
Elderly	150.00
Very dependent elderly	165.00
(defined as those qualifying for the higher rate attendance allowance)	
Mentally handicapped	165.00
Physically disabled who have been so since before pension age	210.00

These levels are increased by £23 within the Greater London area. There is a further allowance of £10.05 for personal expenses which is allowed on top of the limits for all claimants. In April 1990 and August 1990 these rates will increase.

Assessment of how much financial help someone is eligible for with private home fees is undertaken in much the same way as for help with a local authority place, as outlined above. The elderly person will have to fill in a comprehensive financial statement and if they are one of a couple, this will have to apply to both people. For homeowners, the situation is slightly different.

Homeowners will find that the social security department will include any income or capital available from the eventual sale of that house in their financial assessment of someone's worth. The authority can even enforce sale of a house or the taking out of a loan to cover the time it takes to sell in order to get the fees paid. If the elderly person has left a spouse or a carer living in their house, then the authority can use its discretion on forcing the sale of that house.

Elderly who have more than £8,000 in savings but less than £16,000 may qualify for housing benefit to help with the cost of fees in a private home. The local authority will calculate how much of the home's charges are for rent and an elderly person may get some assistance. Also, elderly people in private homes can claim the attendance allowance if they qualify under the rules set out in Chapter 2. However, claiming attendance allowance will affect payment of income support because it is classed as income. However, it is worth investigating to see if the elderly person does benefit financially.

If there is still a shortfall on paying private home fees, once all the resources have been taken into account, the elderly person may find that they are eligible for charitable help, perhaps for reasons of their religion or previous occupation. A useful guide for extra sources of money is *A Guide to Grants for Individuals in Need* by Luke Fitzherbert and Helene Bellofatto, published by the Directory of Social Change.

A member of the older person's family or charity can regularly give up to £5 to an elderly relative without it affecting their income support. After that it is considered income and can affect income support. However, if a family wants to help finance an older member's stay in a private home, they should always get professional advice. It may not always be clear how committed they are to meeting extra costs, either from their own point of view or the private home's. Because the rules on limits for state help for payment of private home fees were changed in 1985, some people who have been claiming since before then are protected claimants and should continue to receive their benefits.

Nursing homes

Nursing homes are the responsibility of the district health authority and must be registered under the Registered Homes Act 1984, regardless of the number of residents. The law also requires that they are run by a qualified doctor or nurse and staffed by professionally qualified people. The category of nursing home covers the full range of residential places for

Residential care

those who need medical care, from private hospitals to small nursing homes.

There is a pilot scheme operating currently in a few parts of the country under which the NHS is opening nursing homes for long term hospitalised patients who need permanent medical care but would benefit from more independence and privacy away from the hospital routine. The district health authority will be able to provide information on whether there is a convenient one locally, but as yet there are few available in the country.

As part of the general move to open up hospital beds where possible, a district health authority will occasionally move a long-stay patient out of hospital and into a private home, often as a temporary measure, and remain responsible for the fees. Again, this scheme does not operate nationwide so if this seems a suitable option enquiries need to be made with the local health authority.

How to pay for nursing homes

As with private residential care homes, the Department of Social Security will help with the cost of nursing home fees, within certain limits.
As at 1 November 1989 the maximum weekly rates for income support towards the cost of nursing home care are:

Maximum weekly rates

	£
Elderly	200.00
Those suffering from mental disorders but not classed as mentally handicapped	200.00
Mentally handicapped	205.00
The terminally ill	245.00
Physically disabled who have been so since before pension age	245.00

Residential care

These limits are increased, as with those for residential care, by £23 in Greater London and the personal expenses allowance is £10.05. In April 1990 and August 1990 these rates will increase. For homes that provide both residential care and nursing care, the onus is on the home manager to decide which treatment the resident receives.

In response to the Griffith's Report on Community Care, the government has announced that from 1991 the local authorities rather than the social services will play a greater role in funding residential care for the elderly. This is likely to make a considerable difference to the benefits available for those entering a local authority home or one run privately or by the voluntary sector.

9 Voluntary provision of residential homes

A further alternative to finding residential care for the elderly is presented by the voluntary sector. For those who do not want to opt for private care but cannot find something suitable in the State system, the major charitable institutions might provide the solution. Further, homes run by non-profit making organisations tend to have any money available ploughed back into those homes, so their standards can be quite high and they can offer a very specialised service.

Many of the existing charitable organisations which provide subsidised housing to the elderly were set up in the Victorian era and consequently have names or images which elderly people may find discouraging. However, the largest organisations have grown with the times and offer a comfortable and professionally run haven for elderly people who need help but do not want to sacrifice their existing quality of life.

Often voluntarily-run homes are a useful resource for people from ethnic or religious groups who would prefer to live with others of the same background. A good example of this is the Nightingale House project in South London, which offers help to elderly Jewish people from sheltered housing to full-time nursing care.

Other homes in the voluntary sector are run by unions or associations and are available to those who have worked in certain industries or professions. For example there are retirement homes for those who were in religious life, or worked for the civil service, or ex-servicemen. Details of homes such as these are available from the relevant union or ex-employers and many organisations will include lists of post-retirement help available for ex-employees in their retirement plans. Even if a previous employer does not offer residential care in retirement, it is still worth making contact because employers can be a source of funding for other accommodation.

Since running residential care homes is an extremely specialised business, many of the big organisations run rather as an umbrella group, offering advice and managing homes on behalf of other smaller voluntary societies.

Abbeyfield homes

One of the biggest of the charitable societies is the Abbeyfield Society. Founded in the 1950s, the Abbeyfield Society has grown to encompass 609 local societies around the UK plus 26 organisations abroad. By the end of 1988 they housed 8,134 elderly people in this country in over 1,000 properties. The initial aim of Abbeyfield was to provide a family lifestyle for a small number of active, elderly people in purpose-built or converted houses around the UK. The residents have their own rooms, usually bed-sitting rooms with limited cooking and washing facilities, into which they can put their own furniture and belongings. The resident housekeeper in each Abbeyfield house cooks one or two main meals a day, depending on the house, and the residents eat together as a family. Apart from that, Abbeyfield residents can be as independent as they wish.

The Society has now expanded into offering extra-care households for elderly residents who need a little more help with day-to-day personal tasks. There are now over 40 extra-care houses in the Abbeyfield Society. They tend to have more residents than the residential homes and are equipped with professional staff and facilities for the frail elderly who need nursing care or just 24 hour attention.

Anyone can apply for a place in an Abbeyfield home. Residents pay a weekly charge to cover the running costs of the house, including fuel bills, community charge etc, and can apply for social security to help with this. The charge tends to be lower than that found in the private sector because much of Abbeyfield's funding comes from charitable giving or funding available through the Housing Corporation. The costs in the extra-care houses can obviously be higher but again there should be social security support available for anyone who is unable to meet the fees.

Because of Abbeyfield's experience in running residential homes for the elderly they also act as managers for some of the smaller voluntary organisations' properties. If you contact the Society, they should be able to point you in the direction of other voluntarily-run residential homes in the area, if they are unable to help you themselves. In some areas, the Society is working with local authorities or health authorities to provide jointly-run housing for the elderly. Details from the Abbeyfield Society. (See Appendix.)

Distressed Gentlefolk's Aid Association

Another large charitable organisation aimed at helping the elderly is The Distressed Gentlefolk's Aid Association. Founded in 1897, the title is a reflection of its Victorian past and need not discourage would-be applicants. Applications are dealt with in a 'reasonably liberal way' to quote the DGAA's literature.

The DGAA runs 14 homes in total. Four are residential care homes aimed at those who are still fit and active and who want to maintain a degree of independence. Four are a mixture of nursing and residential care, offering nursing help to those who need it. Four more offer full-time nursing care and the remaining two offer sheltered accommodation for those who can still live a totally independent life. The DGAA charges a maximum fee for its homes, £170 a week for residential care or £315 for nursing care. However, no-one will be turned away if they cannot afford the full fee. Fees are scaled down for those with lower incomes, although everyone who is entitled is expected to apply for help from social security, and everyone is left with personal spending money, however much they are contributing to the cost of their place.

The DGAA does require a medical examination before admission to their homes and the decision does rest with the homes committee. The Association will not take applications from the blind, those who are in danger of becoming blind, the mentally confused or those who have a history of psychiatric disorders or alcoholism. The DGAA also provides occasional funding for someone who has financial difficulties and the organisation can help with the odd emergency payment in times of crisis, so even if you are just seeking sources of financial help, it is worth contacting them. More specific details are available from The Distressed Gentlefolk's Aid Association. (See Appendix.)

Almshouses

If you travel around the villages and towns of Great Britain, most have a row of neat almshouses still standing. These are a relic from centuries past when large landowners provided accommodation for their staff when they retired. Many are still run as a charity for the local elderly in need and some are still restricted to the terms of the original benefactor's bequest as laid out in a trust. The right to live in an almshouse may still be limited to those who have worked on a local estate, or for the local church or school, for instance. Almshouses are usually supplied rent free, but occasionally there is a regular charge to cover upkeep and maintenance. Most are modernised and some have more of a sheltered housing approach in that a warden is provided to keep a neighbourly eye on tenants. For more details on almshouses, contact the National Association of Almshouses. (See Appendix.)

There are hundreds of other sources of voluntarily aided residential homes for the elderly. Here we have attempted to list a few of the main ones and give you pointers on how to find out about others. Other areas to try are the local library, Citizens' Advice Bureau or local office of Age Concern plus the council's own housing department.

10 Medical and nursing care

The cost of long-term care of someone who needs full-time medical treatment can be quite considerable. Providing 24 hour trained medical care and facilities is an expensive business. Because of the stretched resources of the National Health Service much of the medical care available for the elderly in a hospital is likely to be limited to fulfilling the immediate needs of someone undergoing surgery or who is completely dependent upon hospital facilities. Beyond that, the bulk of medical care for elderly people is farmed out to the voluntary or private sector or to you, the relatives.

Nursing homes

Nursing homes, however they are funded, vary considerably in the amount of nursing care they can give. Some can only look after somebody who is relatively mobile while others can provide medical attention whatever the patient's condition and can nurse residents through until the end. This is something to consider when an elderly relative is choosing a nursing home. A new approach to care for the elderly has seen the development of residential homes that can help residents right the way through from their fairly active years to when they need permanent medical care, without them having to move.

In some areas, the NHS have set up specialist homes that are attached to hospitals and can provide any amount of medical care needed. In the voluntary sector, some of the big charitable organisations such as Abbeyfields are building 'extra-care' units which can provide more nursing care than their other homes.

Care centres

A division of the private medical insurers Private Patient's Plan runs eight nursing care centres and three closer care properties around England on this principle. In PPP-Beaumont's centres the closer care properties are simply privately owned sheltered accommodation for the elderly or disabled. However, as the properties are located next to the nursing care centres, the services available can stretch to complete nursing care and services while the resident stays in their own flat. The nursing care centres themselves are effectively private hospitals where an elderly person can receive long-term nursing care. The closer care properties are around £50,000 to £70,000 to buy and the weekly service charge is on a scale from £60 to £200 depending on the level of services needed. PPP-Beaumont's Nursing Homes cost between £330-£350 a week.

Another private medical insurer, BUPA, runs nursing homes for the elderly, usually based within close proximity of a BUPA private hospital.

Private health insurance schemes

Admission into hospital can be a difficult process if the medical need of an elderly person is something that calls for fairly immediate hospital treatment but does not require a long-term hospital stay. It is estimated that the waiting lists for NHS hospitals have a million people on them and over half of these people are over 55. The problems within the

78 Medical and nursing care

National Health Service have inspired many people recently to look at alternative forms of providing health cover for themselves and their families. Around ten per cent of the population currently subscribes to a private health insurance scheme. The majority of these people are under 60, but about five per cent are estimated to be within the retirement age range.

In the 1989 Budget, the Chancellor announced that the government would introduce tax relief on private medical insurance for people aged over 60. This is obviously only an advantage for people who pay tax and have the income to pay for private medical insurance in the first instance. However, one advantage is that the tax relief is not limited to the person who is the beneficiary of the policy. This means that if you are a taxpayer you can take out and pay for a medical insurance policy for an elderly relative and claim the tax relief yourself.

At the present time only one private health insurance company runs a health policy specifically for the retired. This is the Private Patients Plan's Retirement Health Policy. Under this scheme the insured can 'jump the queue' by visiting a private specialist and hospital if the State alternative is not immediately available. Specialist's fees are only covered if the insured person has to go into hospital. If it will be more than six weeks before the insured can get into a NHS hospital, the insured can go into a private hospital or a NHS pay bed. If there is a bed free within six weeks in the NHS hospital, the insured receives £18 a night up to a maximum 180 nights tax-free payment.

The limits under the policy are £6,500 for in-patient treatment, daycare treatment or out-patient surgical procedures. The limit increases to £13,000 for open-heart surgeries. Treatment at some of London's most expensive private hospitals carries a £525 excess which the insured has to pay. Monthly subscription rates start at £14.45 for those aged under 64 and rise in stages to £47 for those aged 80 and over. Subscriptions can be paid annually or quarterly if preferred.

An elderly person can also be included on PPP's Family Health Plan. This is an extensive private medical insurance policy for the whole family and the person who takes out the insurance can include someone up to 80 and over. However, the premiums for someone in that age group run from £112.55 to £165.55 a month, so this is not an option that would be taken up by everybody.

BUPA also offers a form of private health insurance to retired people. Those aged up to 74 can take out a Budget BUPA Scheme which guarantees hospital treatment within five weeks.

Someone who is considering taking out private medical insurance when the beneficiaries are in their retirement years needs to read the policy quite closely. Private medical insurance can be the solution if an elderly person's medical needs are quite simple, an operation or short period of hospitalisation for instance. Most schemes will cover the cost of immediate needs such as these, but none will cover the cost of long-term medical care for sufferers of chronic illnesses, such as dementia or arthritis.

The exclusions on private health policies usually include any illnesses which have already been diagnosed when the policy is taken out. Convalescent care is often excluded and the cost of renal dialysis is unlikely to be covered. You may also find there is a more limited choice of treatments available under the policy.

The health insurers will usually review their premium rates at least once a year, and increases in the cost of cover can be quite hefty. If you decide that taking out private medical insurance is a good solution, you need to be certain that you can afford to continue with it. Remember that as someone gets older their medical needs are likely to get more extensive and therefore more expensive. Paying for medical care for an elderly person can be very expensive and continuing that payment over a long period of time would drain even the largest resources. It is estimated that the cost involved in a long-term stay in hospital per bed in a geriatric ward is approximately £200 per night.

Private nursing

However, one solution is the provision of nursing in the home. To do this privately, through an agency, a nurse is likely to cost around £10 an hour. This means that employing a private nurse through an agency for a night shift of 10 hours will cost £100 a day, £700 a week. If you can find a local nurse who will work directly for you, this fee could be reduced to maybe between £5 and £7 an hour, but it is still a substantial amount of money. Under some private medical insurance schemes, subscribers can get a discount on the cost of home nursing. For further details on obtaining private nursing services contact your local office of the British Nursing Association.

Medical care for the terminally ill

Hospices

A further option which is only open to those who are terminally ill, is a hospice. The hospice movement has grown enormously in the past 20 years and provides an alternative form of care to that on offer in the State or private sector.

Hospices aim to look after the whole body of terminally ill patients, including helping with their emotional and spiritual needs and those of their families. Drugs are prescribed only to help control pain or the uncomfortable symptoms of a serious illness. Hospice units tend to be as small as is economical, allowing patients to maintain as much dignity and privacy as they want.

It is estimated that 20 per cent of all deaths are caused by cancer, and it is usually cancer patients, of all ages, who are treated in hospices. The pioneering work of Dame Cicely Saunders at St Joseph's Hospice in East London which was one of the first such institutions in this country resulted in a small boom in the provision of hospice care rather than hospital for the terminally ill.

Generally, hospices are run by the voluntary sector, including anything from a small local charity to the national charities such as Sue Ryder or the Marie Curie Memorial Foundation. Because of the high cost of running hospices and their voluntary funding, there are not enough hospices available around the country. The highest proportion are based in the South-East.

Their success in the treatment of the terminally ill, however, has attracted the attention of the NHS. Some areas can now provide hospice care through a liaison between the district health authority and the voluntary sector. For instance, in some areas, the National Society for Cancer Relief has paid the capital cost of setting up a hospice unit but the running costs are paid for by the NHS.

Some District Health Authorities have a permanent arrangement with a voluntarily-run hospice to use and fund a certain number of beds, so if your elderly relative is terminally ill, you may find that a place is offered in a hospice unit through the NHS.

Home units

A further development from the hospice movement is the foundation of 'home units' which rely on assistance from the State and the voluntary sector. These are usually attached to a local hospital and are made up of a team of medical workers who can monitor, treat and nurse someone with a long-term illness in their own home. The nursing provision under these schemes is often drawn from the voluntary sector, although in some areas the District Nurse and her team are involved. Doctors are either the patient's GP or from the local hospital. Voluntary nursing provision usually comes through the Marie Curie Memorial Foundation, whose voluntary nurses sit with cancer patients all around the clock.

A further example of the voluntary sector working with the State is the Cancer Relief Macmillan Fund's nurses. Macmillan nurses work in community services or hospital based teams within the NHS. For the first three years their services and specialist training in caring for cancer patients are paid for by the charity. After that, although the NHS takes up their employment, Macmillan nurses can still use the back-up resources of the Cancer Relief charity and attend regular seminars on new developments in cancer treatment.

Treatment within the patients own home is a much cheaper way for the State to fund care for someone who is dying and for the patients it means that they have a familiar team looking after them and are treated in familiar surroundings.

Unfortunately, because hospices and home units provide a popular choice of treatment for someone who is terminally ill, it can be difficult to get a bed in one. Because terminal illness can strike at any age group, hospices are not limited to the care of the elderly and you may even find that an elderly person does not have priority for a bed.

The local GP, District Health Authority or the national charities which work in cancer relief will be able to tell you if there is a hospice near you, or whether there is a home unit scheme operating in your area.

11 Legal aspects of illness

If an elderly person becomes so mentally or physically incapacitated that they are unable to make decisions for themselves or look after their own affairs, it can become extremely distressing. The aim of this chapter is to outline what rights an elderly person has under these circumstances, and what rights you can claim as a relative. In the next chapter we will outline what options there are for the long term medical care of someone who needs skilled nursing permanently.

As a family in this situation you will want to make the best decisions, most in keeping with what your relative would want, and providing them with the best quality of life possible, whatever their condition. However, it may be the first time that you realise that your parent has become dependent upon you, rather as a child is dependent upon its parents and that you are expected to know what options are available and how to cope on a practical level while emotionally feeling very distressed.

Illness

It is very rare for an elderly person to be pushed into complete loss of independence through a legal move. This would only happen in extreme circumstances under use of the Mental Health Act or s47 of the National Assistance Act. The first covers a situation whereby someone is received under the 'guardianship' of the Social Services in order to protect themselves or others. It is very rarely used but can happen if an elderly person is not coping at home, is behaving in a strange fashion and is dangerous, either to themselves or others. If this happens to an elderly relative of yours, you can object and the matter must be referred to the county court before the process can be completed. Once someone has been admitted to the guardianship process, it continues for six months before a renewal is needed. An appointed guardian, usually someone from the Social Services department or someone appointed by them, can dictate where the patient lives and that they are available for medical assessment. However, the guardian cannot force a patient to have medical treatment and the patient can appeal against the guardianship order.

Under the National Assistance Act, s47 allows the forcible removal of an elderly person from their home and placement in residential care, usually because they are deemed to be at risk through not being able to cope on their own, or because they desperately need medical attention in a hospital and refuse to enter one.

The aim of both of these laws is to protect the mental and physical well-being of someone who is no longer capable of looking after themseves properly. However, if you as a family have been taking on the burden of care for that person, you should be involved throughout the decision-making process on their future. Unfortunately, you have few legal rights to insist on being involved but generally, doctors and the social services would rather include you when trying to determine the future for your elderly relative.

Unless elderly people have been specifically treated under either of these two laws, they are deemed to be independent and have the right to know what treatment they are receiving and to refuse it if they wish. As many elderly people are not seriously disturbed enough to qualify under the Mental Health Act, simply a little confused and forgetful, it can fall to their relatives to ensure that they receive adequate and caring treatment as they would have wished. Sometimes it is difficult to know what that person would have wanted and now there is a new concept in planning ahead for just such an eventuality.

The Living Will

The 'Living Will' started in the USA, where in many States it is legally binding. However, in the UK it can only be used as an indication of someone's wishes in the event of their physical or mental breakdown, and as such it can be very useful.

The idea is that while someone is in complete control of all their faculties they write down their wishes for their treatment if that situation ever changed. Usually, people state clearly whether they would want their lives to be prolonged by the use of artificial life support methods if their condition was irreversible or other such matters. Understandably, many people are loathe to discuss such an event, but a living Will does give the next of kin and their medical attendants an indication of their wishes in the event of a complete physical or mental breakdown.

Consent to treatment

One of the problems that may occur if you have an elderly relative who is hospitalised or resident in a nursing home, is that you may not agree with the amount of medication being administered, which in some cases may increase their confusion or leave them lethargic and sleepy.

The law requires that anyone, not committed under the Mental Health Act, who is going to be treated for any illness gives their consent before treatment, except in cases of emergency. However, often, with an elderly confused person consent is assumed, and the simple act of taking medication without complaining can be considered enough consent. If you are worried about the medication a relative is being prescribed, you should try and talk to their doctor. If your relative is in hospital, the doctors are governed by various codes of practice on their prescriptive powers. In nursing homes, apart from the rules governing the doctors' powers, the voluntary code of practice Home Life (more clearly outlined in Chapter 8) has clear guidelines for managing staff on the question of prescribing drugs. For instance, drugs should not be used to control patients, keeping them from normal social activities etc.

If you are worried about any aspect of the medical treatment of a relative who is not able to complain for themselves, do not be frightened to ask questions. Unfortunately, you do not have the legal right to decide for a confused person in most cases, but that person does have rights and if you are prepared to act on their behalf you may find that the staff will be happy to include you in any decision-making processes.

Financial matters

Another area that can be fraught with problems once an elderly person has become too frail to make decisions, is what happens to their money and their estate. This can be a particularly unpleasant problem because no-one would want any suggestion, either from authorities or other relatives, that an elderly person's estate is being managed or dealt with in a way they would not have wanted. Unfortunately, the matter cannot be left unattended. Many elderly people's treatment and care are being financed out of their estates and someone needs to organise their finances.

If someone is resident in a nursing home but wishes to continue to manage their own money, they are entitled to do so. No home has the right to keep an elderly person's pension book and simply give them their spending money, and this is covered in the Home Life code of practice.

Agents

If elderly people do not want or are unable to continue collecting their own pension or benefits, they can appoint an agent. This is likely to be a relative, friend or neighbour. It should not be someone connected with their nursing home or hospital. The only exception to this is in local authority homes where, if the residents wish, the authority can become the signing agent and cash the cheques on their behalf. To appoint an agent, the elderly person signs the printed statement on the back of their pension or benefit slip in front of an independent witness and the agent is then allowed to collect their pension. The agents are only empowered to collect it and hand it over, they are not allowed to spend it or keep it without further authority from the true owner. If an agent is likely to be needed for a long time, the Department of Social Security can issue an agency card which names the agent officially.

If your elderly relative has suddenly become too ill to organise this, but social security payments are needed to continue to fund the care, the Department of Social Security can take a statement of circumstances from you and obtain reports and pay the money to you or somebody else responsible. This can be done for a temporary period only.

Appointees

If the condition of the elderly person deteriorates further, social security payments can be made directly to an appointee, although payment remains in the claimant's name. An appointee can collect the money and spend it, subject to strict rules that the money is spent in the interests of the claimant. An appointee must also tell the social security department of any change in circumstances of the claimant and can apply for further benefits on their behalf.

Would-be appointees must write to the local social security department and the claimant is either visited or a medical report prepared on why they are unable to claim payments themselves. Appointees are usually interviewed on their suitability for the role. Ideally, appointees are relatives or friends of the claimant, although sometimes the manager of a nursing home or hospital administrator fills the role. The code of practice Home Life does not recommend that a nursing home proprietor becomes the appointee for a resident.

Because there is no requirement for appointees to furnish proper accounts on how they are spending a claimant's money, the system can be open to abuses. If your elderly relative is using one of the nursing home staff as an appointee, find out how the money is being spent and check that, once the fees have been paid, the rest is not going into a general pool. If it is at all practical, it is better to become the appointee yourself or find a volunteer, perhaps from the local Age Concern office, to undertake the task. If you find a registered nursing home that is behaving in an unscrupulous way with residents' money, report them to the district health authority or the local authority, in the case of a residential care home.

Powers of attorney and the formation of trusts

The power of attorney gives someone else complete freedom to look after a person's affairs within the framework of the law. To act as a further safeguard many people appoint two people as their attorneys, and they have to act jointly on that person's estate.

The power of attorney can only be granted by someone who is in full possession of their mental faculties and is revoked once the donor becomes mentally incapable. In practice, many people continue to act as attorneys for someone else's affairs whatever the subsequent mental state of the donor. However, the attorney is personally responsible for anything done during the period when the donor was mentally incapable. If for instance, another relative makes a complaint about the handling of the estate, the attorney is held responsible.

When someone sets up a power of attorney, they can specifically outline the limitations of their attorney's powers and while they are still mentally capable can cancel the power at any time, but would be well advised to notify all the relevant people (bank, solicitor etc) in writing. Because so many attorneys were continuing to act for people whose mental faculties were impaired, the government introduced the Enduring Power of Attorney Act. Under this Act, if the attorney considers that the donor is becoming mentally incapable they must register the Enduring Power of Attorney with the Court of Protection and must notify the donor and their relatives that they have done so.

An alternative to setting up a power of attorney is for the older person to put all their assets into a trust by a deed of trust, drawn up and administered by their solicitors. The trust needs to be drawn up while the older person has full command of his faculties and can be very detailed on the planned management of his estate. The appointed trustees can administer that estate on behalf of the older person, whatever happens to them. Professional trustees, such as solicitors, will charge for their services.

The Court of Protection

This is an ancient court that exists to protect the assets of someone who is mentally incapacitated. Because it initially

90 Legal aspects of illness

appears very confusing and bureaucratic, many people continue to act as an attorney under the Power of Attorney rulings, rather than advance the matter on to the Court of Protection. However, it is there to safeguard the interests of someone who has mental problems. Because it only applies to people with an estate above a certain size, most of the people under the court's protection are in the elderly age group. Application to the Court of Protection should always be made but if the assets are under £5,000 the court is likely to issue a summary order, rather than appoint a receiver. In the case of someone who has assets of over £5,000 which can be very simply handled it is likely that the court will order that the assets are cashed and used to cover the patient's needs. For more complicated affairs, the court usually appoints a receiver for that person's estate. The receiver is expected to handle the assets as the patient would have done, if they were able.

A receiver can be a relative or a solicitor, although if the receiver appoints a solicitor to help them with receivership duties they have to pay the bill themselves. The receiver is required to make a report to the court, usually once a year, on what he has done with the estate. For the first few years, at least, the receiver will have to present accounts for the estate and he is expected to visit the patient and check that they are kept as comfortable as possible. If the patient is hospitalised the court sends an annual questionnaire on the patient's comfort and financial means. The court can also send a visitor of their own to check that all is in order if the patient is living in a home or out of a hospital for some reason.

12 Boosting income and capital

Having done your assessment of your elderly relatives' needs and resources, you might feel that they still have a relatively low income on which to meet these needs. However, it is possible that they are living in something which is wholly-owned and of considerable value—ie their home.

Despite the recent setbacks to the UK's property market a considerable proportion of older people live in houses on which they have no mortgage and which have a high capital value. Nowadays it is possible for older people to tap that locked-up capital and boost their incomes without having to move house.

In order to get the most benefit from these schemes, the homeowners need to be at least 70. Generally, the older the homeowner, the higher the income or capital sum which can be generated.

Home Income Plans

The principal method under which this is possible is a Home Income Plan. Also known as a mortgage annuity, the Home Income Plan allows an elderly person to take out a mortgage on part of the capital value of their house and buy an annuity with the lump sum. This will provide an income for life.

They can remain living in the house for as long as they wish and on death, the mortgage is paid off and the difference in the capital value goes into the estate.

Because of the benefit of tax relief on mortgages, the maximum amount someone can release through a Home Income Plan is usually £30,000. As, generally, women live longer than men, a man will get a higher income from an annuity than a woman. Further, the older someone is when they take out an annuity, the higher the income provided. This is because the capital sum has to be stretched further for someone who has a long life ahead of them. As a consequence, Home Income Plans are only really suitable for those aged over 70.

However, to give you an idea of the amount of income available under the plan, a loan of £30,000 would buy a woman of 75 an annuity that would pay her just over £3,500 a year for the rest of her life.

Tax and the Home Income Plan

Because the homeowner is buying an income, they need to be sure that it won't have a disastrous effect upon their tax status. The loan is used to purchase an annuity, the interest receives tax relief on the loan up to £30,000 as with any other mortgage.

Similarly, as the Inland Revenue regard this is as a return of capital only a small part of the annuity is taxable. Tax is normally deducted at source so the income arrives net of tax for those who are basic rate taxpayers. For those who aren't taxpayers, the income may still be within the income tax age allowances for retired people.

Age Allowances 1990/91

	Over 65	Over 75
Single people	£3,670	£3,820
Couples	£2,145	£2,185

For instance, someone who receives a State pension of £43.60 a week as their only income would have an annual income of £2,267 which means that they would still not have to pay tax even if the taxable 'interest element' was £1,133.

At the other end of the scale once a retired person's income is over £12,300 a year, the age allowance is reduced on a sliding scale until it is back down to the basic personal allowance. If someone has a large income in retirement and tax is being assessed in this way, a Home Income Plan can actually cut the tax bill. This is because when the total taxable income is being assessed the gross mortgage interest on the loan is deducted—resulting in a lowering of income for tax purposes.

Additionally, for those with a potential Inheritance Tax liability, a Home Income Plan can reduce the liability as the loan is treated as a debt on the estate.

Anyone considering taking out a Home Income Plan needs to get advice on how this will affect their tax position.

Home Reversion Schemes

A Home Reversion Scheme is similar to a Home Income Plan in that it gives an elderly person the opportunity to release some of the capital in their house and obtain a lump sum or buy an income.

However, with a Home Reversion Scheme, the homeowner actually *sells* the house to a company and retains only the right to live there for their lifetime. The price paid for the house under these schemes tends to be considerably lower than the market value. Also any increase in the capital value of the property after it has been sold goes to the company running the Home Reversion Scheme, not to the ex-homeowner. A few schemes now available allow someone to take out a partial reversion, keeping a proportion of the capital value of the property when it is finally sold.

The advantages of the Home Reversion Scheme are that some are available to younger retired people, in some cases as low as 60. Also, there is usually no maximum limit on the value of the properties and the homeowner may choose to take his capital as a lump sum or an annuity.

However, something to bear in mind if the elderly person has a very limited income is that under the terms of a Home Reversion Scheme he still has to pay towards the maintenance of the property plus a rent for continuing to live there.

Retired people who are interested in taking out a Home Reversion Scheme need to be fully aware that they will have *signed away their homes*—they can no longer include them among their assets. They will not be part of the estate on death.

The fine details of the schemes vary considerably from company to company—if your elderly relative is considering one, make sure they get proper legal and financial advice.

Other possibilities

There are other schemes aimed at helping to provide an income for elderly people.

Interest-only loans

Some building societies will give an interest-only loan against the capital value of a house. There is also the option to roll-up the interest into the total debt which is then paid off when the property is finally sold. These loans can prove extremely expensive in the long run. It is not impossible for the loan to become equal to, or even overtake, the capital value of the house, particularly in times of high interest rates. Once again, anyone considering one of these schemes should get very good legal and financial advice and be completely clear on how much the eventual debt could be.

Investment bonds

Another scheme is an investment bond income scheme. Under this the homeowner mortgages the property for part of its value and the lump sum raised is put into an investment bond. This is likely to be invested in income-producing equities or fixed interest securities. If someone is considering taking out one of these they should ponder on the stockmarket crash of 1987 and the subsequent stockmarket jitters. There is little security in depending on this for total income.

Other points to bear in mind

When considering releasing some capital from a property to produce an income for an elderly person bear in mind just how the new income will affect any current receipt of social security benefits.

Most of the benefits outlined in Chapter 2 are only available to people with limited savings and a very low income. It is unlikely that they could continue to receive benefits if they had released some of their capital and they would need to judge whether they were better off with State benefits rather than the payments from an annuity or other scheme.

13 Your own pension arrangements

The first 12 chapters in this book have looked at ways and means of helping older folk, but it is worth pausing at this juncture to consider your own position.

If you are coming up to retirement and your parents are still alive, take a good long look at how they're doing. Ask yourself some questions: are they fit and active and how much longer will that last? Do they have enough money for their needs? Is where they live still suitable for them? If suddenly they needed financial help or caring help, would you be able to shoulder those responsibilities? What will you be able to do to help those you love once *you* have retired and are also living on a fixed income?

In the light of these questions you might want to cast a fresh eye over your own pension arrangements.

Pensions

As you will know, the pension industry in the UK has been going through something of a revolution over the past few years. The Government pledged to encourage employees to take responsibility upon themselves for funding their retirement and consequently changed the laws to encourage people into private pension provision.

Your own pension arrangements

There are various excellent publications on the pensions maze which will explain fully what the new legislation means and what your options are. However, here are a few suggestions for ways to boost your post-retirement income and capital when you are approaching the end of your working life.

Occupational pension schemes

Those in an occupational pension scheme, run by their employers, are allowed tax relief on contributions which represent up to 15 per cent of their salary. If you are retiring in a few years and not contributing anything like that much, one option available to you to bump up your final pension is to boost the amount of salary you put into it while you are still working. Many people find that they have a lot more cash in their later years of working because their children have left home or they have paid off their mortgages. If you feel you can pay more into investments for your future you have several options through an occupational pension scheme.

Additional voluntary contributions

You can boost your pension by paying additional voluntary contributions (AVCs) through your present pension scheme or set up an independent extra plan through which you can make free-standing additional voluntary contributions (FSAVCs).

If you choose the latter, you are entitled to make contributions net of tax at source. This means that if you are within the basic tax bracket of 25 per cent you can make a £10.00 contribution and pay only £7.50—the rest will be rebated back to your pension. If you are a higher rate taxpayer, you can claim tax relief at 25 per cent and arrange for the rest to be rebated through your income tax assessment in the normal way, or through changing your PAYE coding.

You are allowed to do this in an occupational scheme up to certain limits. If on retirement the limit is exceeded, you will get the excess back as a lump sum but you will have to pay tax on it. Payments from an occupational pension aren't limited to providing a regular income: on retirement you can take a substantial lump sum out of the fund totally tax-free.

For further advice on your pension, you should talk to your salary or pension office at work or a financial adviser.

Personal pensions

The limits on contributions to your pension are even higher if you have a personal pension. This option is not available to those who are members of an occupational scheme. In a personal pension plan, tax relief is allowable on contributions up to 35 per cent of your salary once you have reached the age of 56 and 40 per cent of salary once you have reached age 61.

However, there is in effect an upper limit on contributions to personal pensions plans in that earnings above £64,800 per annum with effect from April 1990 (to be increased annually in line with the Retail Prices Index) are disregarded.

Contribution Limit As Percentage Of Net Earnings 1990/91

Age	Limit %	Maximum Contribution pa
36–45	20	£10,500
46–50	25	£12,000
51–55	30	£15,000
56–60	35	£18,000
61 or over	40	£21,000

The release of a capital sum from a personal pension is not dependent upon your retirement. You can release up to one quarter of the fund as a tax-free lump sum whenever you first start to draw your pension, whether you are still working or not.

Employers are not obliged to contribute towards an employee's personal pension plan: some do, some don't. However, you do have the right to choose what sort of pension you want. If you are in an occupational scheme and decide that you would rather have a personal pension, you can opt out without penalty. Your existing contributions in the occupational scheme will sit tight and wait for your retirement and meanwhile you can boost your retirement funds with a personal pension plan.

There are many books dealing in detail with pensions. One useful book is another Allied Dunbar Money Guide, *Planning Your Pension* and/or *Allied Dunbar Pensions Guide* written by Tony Reardon.

14 Where there's a Will

The question of making a Will must be one of the most often avoided subjects in conversations with older people. According to the General Household Survey in 1986, nearly half of the over-65s had not made a Will. The figure should be much, much lower because whatever our age, planning ahead and organising our affairs in the event of death is essential if we want the best for our families whatever happens.

A lot of people rely on the law to sort out their affairs when they die—'well I want it all to go to my wife anyway' is a fairly common expression. Like most things, it's not quite that simple, as shown later in this chapter. The other common mistake on the subject is: 'Well, I haven't got that much anyway.'

A person's estate includes everything that they leave behind them, including the value of a house or car. It soon mounts up and sensible planning ahead can keep the tax bills down.

Making a Will

This can be done with a solicitor or personally. To be completely certain that your Will is unambiguous and legally correct it is better to use a solicitor. If you have a sizeable estate, you will need to get some financial planning advice as well.

Inheritance tax

Since 1986 estates in England and Wales have been subject to Inheritance Tax. While many may happily believe that IHT only applies to the very wealthy, nothing could be further from the truth.

Inheritance Tax is charged in two bands. The first band is charged at a nil rate up to £128,000—this means that no Inheritance Tax is charged on everything up to that amount and after that Inheritance Tax is chargeable at the rate of 40 per cent.

In order to show how easy it is for an estate to add up to a value well in excess of £128,000, we'll invent Mr Smith.

Mr Smith's assets

House	£130,000
House contents	£ 30,000
Car	£ 3,000
Life assurance policy	£ 5,000
2 weeks timeshare	£ 10,000
Savings and investments	£ 15,000
Mortgage protection policy	£ 20,000
Bank Account/Building Society	£ 7,000
Total gross estate	£220,000
Less Mortgage	£ 20,000
Total net estate	£200,000

If Mr Smith dies he will leave a gross estate of £220,000. The mortgage protection policy would be used to pay off his mortgage leaving a net estate of £200,000.

Mr Smith therefore 'owns' £200,000 net—but regards himself as 'worth' only £22,000 (his bank accounts and his

102 *Where there's a Will*

savings: after all he can't spend the house and contents, and the life policy is only there when he isn't).

The Table below shows how the tax builds up on an estate of £500,000.

Slice of Estate £	Cumulative Total £	% on Slice	Cumulative Tax £
The first 128,000	128,000	Nil	Nil
The next 72,000	200,000	40	28,000
100,000	300,000	40	72,800
100,000	400,000	40	112,800
100,000	500,000	40	152,800

The last table shows how much tax would be payable on Mr Smith's estate.

Slice of Estate £	Cumulative Total £	% on Slice	Cumulative Tax £
The first 128,000	128,000	Nil	Nil
The next 72,000	200,000	40	28,000

As you can see the total potential tax bill is £28,000—almost 15 per cent of the total net value of the estate—frightening, isn't it?

With careful planning it is possible to achieve reductions in the eventual Inheritance Tax burden. One of the major exemptions from Inheritance Tax is that everything left to a spouse does not attract liability to the tax. This is very useful as long as a Will has been written making it clear that the *whole* estate is to go to the spouse.

A financial adviser or solicitor would be likely to recommend re-distributing your capital during your lifetime to cut down on the potential tax liability, perhaps by giving it to your children, or establishing a trust. At present transfers of assets made more than seven years before the transferor's death are exempt from Inheritance Tax.

If you feel that your elderly relative needs advice on leaving their affairs in order, you should encourage them to seek professional help either from a solicitor or accountant.

There are several useful publications on the subject of making a Will, including one in the Allied Dunbar Money Guide series, *Leaving your Money Wisely* by Tony Foreman.

If there is no Will

If your elderly relative dies intestate, that is without making a Will, the law states how the estate should be divided up. The rules of intestacy are not what many people expect:

When there is a surviving partner with children

The surviving partner gets the first £75,000 plus interest plus personal possessions and a life interest in half of the rest of the estate, the other half going to the children.

When there is a surviving partner with no children

The surviving partner gets the first £125,000 plus any interest plus personal possessions and half of the remainder of the estate. The second half goes to any parents, if still alive, if not, then to brothers, sisters or their children if they are still alive. If there are no other relatives, the surviving partner gets the whole estate.

When there is a no surviving partner

The estate is divided between the children if there is no surviving partner and if there are no children, the estate goes to the following in this order: grandchildren, parents, brothers and sisters, grandparents, aunts and uncles, nephews and nieces or cousins.

When there is no Will and no relatives

The Crown generally gets the whole estate. Details from the Treasury Solicitor's Department (BV), Queen Anne's Chambers, 28 Broadway, London SW1H 9JS.

How to be a personal representative

If you are named in a deceased person's Will as their personal representative, then you are the **executor** of the estate. If there is no Will, you are the **administrator**. In the former case, you need to apply for a grant of probate and in the latter, letters of administration in order to organise someone's affairs. A solicitor will be able to help you or you can contact the probate registry office for help.

If the estate is valued at less than £5,000, you might not need to go through the probate office. In this instance, you can get advice from a solicitor or the probate registry office.

As personal representative you are responsible for ensuring that all the deceased's debts, taxes and expenses are paid out of the estate. It is usually a good idea to advertise for any outstanding creditors otherwise the personal representative can be found liable for any debts that were not paid back on distribution of the estate.

After all the bills and expenses have been paid, the remainder can be divided out as the Will or rules of intestacy direct.

Deeds of Variation

Strangely enough, this is not necessarily the end of the matter. If someone named in the Will, a **beneficiary**, does not wish to receive their inheritance (perhaps for reasons of their own estate planning) it is possible to vary the deceased's Will provided all beneficiaries and executors are in agreement with the variation.

It is not uncommon for a grandparent to have made a Will leaving money to a child who has since grown-up. Their son or daughter may now wish to see the money from the estate go directly in turn to the grandchildren. A Deed of Variation can achieve this. However, once again, legal and financial advice ought to be taken in these matters and the Deed must be finalised within two years of probate being obtained.

15 When someone dies

Death is the great leveller, it will come to us all and inevitably, sooner or later, we will see it happen to those we love.

However prepared one is for the death of an elderly person, it still comes as a shock. In these modern days where death is kept very separate from normal family life, the first death most of us are likely to be involved with is of someone with whom we were close.

Often, elderly people cope with the idea of death better than their younger relatives. Many want to make sure that their affairs are in order and their wishes for funeral arrangements are clear. This means that you need to listen to them, talk with them and together become prepared for the event and for carrying out those wishes.

There is an unwritten law that states that the simpler and more natural the act, the more complicated the bureaucracy. Death is no different. We are born into a mass of paperwork and we die with it too. In both cases, we rely on others to sort it out. In this chapter we will look at the practical side, what has to be done in the event of a death and how to ensure that the deceased's wishes are carried out.

What to do

If death happens at home, the first person to contact is the doctor. In England and Wales, when someone dies peacefully the doctor who attended the death, or who normally looked after the deceased, will issue a medical certificate in a sealed envelope addressed to the Registrar. The medical certificate shows the cause of death. The doctor will also issue a formal notice which confirms that he has signed the medical certificate and explains how to register the death. If you are the next of kin or the executor of the estate, the doctor is likely to give these papers to you.

If the deceased died of a natural illness but the doctor wants to know more about it he may ask the next of kin for permission for a post-mortem.

If the death was a result of an accident, injury, industrial disease, surgery or anaesthetics administered during surgery or the dead person was not seen by a doctor during the 14 days before his death, the doctor will refer the death to the Coroner. The Coroner is a doctor or lawyer who makes enquiries into somebody's death if they died under any of the circumstances listed above.

Having done his investigations, the Coroner can issue the paperwork necessary for the death to be registered (Form 100). If the death of your relative has been referred to the Coroner for some reason, you can find out more details from his office which can be contacted either through the hospital, if the relative died there, or through the local police station.

Registering the death

If the death has not been referred to the Coroner and you have the necessary paperwork, you must register the death within five days. This has to be done with the Registrar of Births, Deaths and Marriages in the area in which the death occurred. You can find the address under Registration in the phone book or ask the doctor or local post office.

108 When someone dies

When you visit the Registrar, you will need to take either the medical certificate from the doctor or the Pink Form 100 from the Coroner confirming the cause of death, plus any War Pension order book or medical card, if the deceased had one. You will need to be able to tell the Registrar:

- the date and place of death

- the deceased's last permanent address

- the deceased's name in full—including maiden name in the case of a married women

- the deceased's date and place of birth

- the occupation of the deceased plus the name and occupation of his or her spouse

- whether the deceased was in receipt of a pension or allowance from public funds

- if a spouse survives the deceased, you will need to give the date of birth of that person.

Once all the details have been provided, the Registrar will give you a certificate for burial or cremation (if the Coroner has not already provided one). He will also give you a certificate of registration of death which has to be filled in, if applicable, and sent to the social security office. He will also supply details of widow's benefits where appropriate.

The Registrar can also supply a death certificate which is a certified copy of the entry in the death register. There will be a charge for this but you are likely to need at least one to sort out the deceased's affairs, for instance notifying an insurance company or sorting out pension claims or other investments.

Medical aspects

If your elderly relative wished to donate parts of their body for transplant purposes you must inform the doctor immediately. The vital organs can only be used for transplants if they are removed from the body, within half an hour of death, and the corneas (part of the eye) have to be removed within 12 hours. If someone has made it particularly clear before dying that they did not want to donate any part of their body, relatives cannot overrule this.

If your elderly relative wanted to donate their entire body for medical purposes, contact the Anatomy Office of the local medical school or HM Inspector of Anatomy. If they accept the body, they can keep it for teaching purposes for up to two years. After that they will let the family know that the body can either be released for a funeral or the medical school will organise it themselves.

Moving a body

A body cannot be moved out of England and Wales without permission of the Coroner. Permission has to be applied for at least four days before the body is moved. The Coroner makes his investigations and then issues a Removal Notice, part of which is sent to the Registrar. So, if your relative wished to be buried in Scotland but died in England, you will have to contact the Coroner for permission. Coroners can either be contacted through the hospital, if that is where your relative died, or you can get the number from the local police station.

What to do if someone dies abroad

If the death occurs abroad, it must be registered according to the local regulations and also with the British Consul. You can either arrange a local burial or cremation or bring the body back. This can be very expensive, but some travel insurance policies or health insurance policies cover the cost of this, particularly if an elderly person is travelling with a company that specialises in travel for the elderly. If you know that your relative would want to be buried or cremated in England, you will need to contact the British Consul in the area where they died. To bring a body back into England and Wales you will need the local death certificate plus a local authorisation to move the body. You will also need a Certificate of No Liability to Register from the British Registrar in whose area you plan to bury or cremate the body. The local British Consul will arrange that a record of the death abroad is added to the records in England.

In the case where the body has been brought back from abroad and is to be cremated, you will need consent from the Home Office. Write to the Home Office and mark the envelope CREMATION URGENT.

Arranging a funeral

Having organised the paperwork, the next step is the funeral arrangements. The Office of Fair Trading recently investigated the funeral business and agreed a Code of Conduct with the National Association of Funeral Directors. If you choose a funeral director who is a member of the NAFD, he must abide by this Code which ensures that costs are clear and not exceeded without your permission.

Feelings run very high on the question of funerals. Most people feel very strongly on the subject, some wanting a full formal funeral and burial, others are happy with a simple cremation and remembrance service. If you have had an opportunity to talk about it with your relatives you will have some idea of what their wishes were. If you haven't, look through their papers to see if there is any indication of what they had planned. You may find that they have a Cremation Society Certificate, which gives a clear guideline on their choice plus a possible reduction in the cost. Or they may have booked a burial space in a churchyard or cemetery.

It is possible that the deceased had pre-paid for their funeral by taking one of the plans available nowadays. Under these, anyone can arrange for their funeral in advance, paying in instalments or a lump sum. If they had one of these plans, you will find a certificate and contact number included among the person's papers. For more details on pre-paid funeral plans contact Age Concern or the National Association of Funeral Directors. You should also check with the deceased's solicitors to see if there was a Will and whether this included details of their wishes for a funeral.

If there was no pre-paid arrangement, you will need the services of a funeral director. Ideally, you should get two estimates for the cost and bear in mind the Code of Conduct operated by members of the NAFD.

To arrange a funeral you will need to give the funeral director the Certificate for Burial or Cremation given to you by the Registrar, or the equivalent paperwork from the Coroner's office. Once you have decided whether your relative would have preferred a burial or cremation, the funeral director will give you more forms to be filled in.

For cremation, the funeral director will give you an Application Form, which you have to fill in. If the death was not referred to the Coroner or did not happen abroad, the funeral director will give you two cremation certificates. These must be signed by two different doctors and you will have to pay for them. The final form is a certificate which must be signed by the medical referee at the crematorium.

There is a charge for this. Cremation is usually cheaper than a burial. Most crematoria are run by local authorities. You should have some choice on a religious service and it is usually possible to arrange for a plaque or memorial stone to be placed in the crematorium's grounds. The Church of England has set fees for the cost of a chaplain to conduct a service at a crematorium. The crematorium staff or your funeral director should ask you what you want to do with the ashes. These can be scattered or buried in a local churchyard, with the local vicar's approval, or scattered in a place that held particular importance for the deceased.

Burial can be slightly more difficult. Most urban churchyards and many rural churchyards are full. Unless the deceased has already reserved a space, the next option will be a non-denominational cemetery. The costs of a full church service and burial are usually higher than the cost of a cremation. You have to remember the fees for the Vicar, (again, this is set by the Church of England), the choir or organist, if you have one, and any other costs associated with using a church, such as the cost of flowers or heating.

Paying for a funeral

If the deceased did not have a funeral plan, you might have to pay for the funeral yourself until the estate is finalised. You can discuss this with the funeral director. If you receive social security benefits you may be able to claim the cost of the funeral from the Social Fund, as mentioned in Chapter 2.

The Social Fund will pay for the cost of bringing the body home if the person died within the United Kingdom, the cost of one return trip to arrange or travel to the funeral, the cost of the death certificate, the cost of a plain coffin, transport for the coffin plus one other car for mourners, the cost of a floral arrangement from the person arranging the funeral and the fees for the funeral director, chaplain and organist. If you get a payment from the Social Fund to cover the cost of a simple funeral, you may have to repay it out of the deceased's estate, once it is sorted out.

In the case of the death of a war pensioner who either died from their war injury or received the constant attendance allowance, the State will pay the costs of a simple funeral and this does not have to be repaid out of the estate. A claim must be made within three months of the funeral.

Some company pension schemes or trade unions will contribute towards the cost of the funeral for an ex-employee. Details should be among the deceased's papers.

If the person who died was resident in a local authority home, some councils will organise and pay for the funeral and if they were in hospital, some health authorities will help out. Details are available from the local council office or health authority office.

When somebody dies, their assets are frozen until the estate is sorted out. However, some building societies and the National Savings Department will pay up to £5,000 to help with the cost of the funeral, if you show them the death certificate. Similarly, some insurance companies will make an advance on a life assurance policy on production of the death certificate in order to help with the cost of a funeral.

16 Financial peace of mind

You could be forgiven for feeling rather anxious about retirement by this time. Don't be, it does not have to be that way. Nowadays more and more people are retiring in their 50s with good occupational pension provision and tidy lump sums of capital in their wholly-owned houses—it is a great time to be over 50. At this age people are fit, active and healthy; able to enjoy the good things in life; spending more time with their spouse and following pursuits that got put aside while working. Retirement can be great. The secret is in being prepared, both financially and emotionally.

Once you are prepared you can live life to the full whatever your age or your responsibilities from your 50s upwards. More and more people are living until well into their 80s and enjoying an independent fulfilled life.

There are many books available on planning your own retirement. This one is different. It is aimed at taking into account the needs of your older relatives.

If you are coming up to retirement and have elderly parents, you will need to think of them when planning for yourself. There are many things you can do that will help out in the event of a crisis. Something as simple as ensuring that you have adequate travel insurance when you go on holiday that would cover the cost of cancellation or having to suddenly come home in the event of your parents' illness; or the installation of a personal alarm system in your parents' house or even something simple like a small monthly gift of money to a relative on a restricted income.

Helping them with simple tax planning—especially if they are not taxpayers yet have money invested and paying interest net of basic rate tax. It would be far better to put their money with National Savings where income is paid gross or make sure that the account is clearly paying gross of tax, once composite rate tax (CRT) is abolished in 1991.

Financial planning in this way will improve both your quality of life and theirs. What we all need is—financial peace of mind.

17 A final thought

Much of this book could be a little depressing, but it should be remembered that older people have a wealth of experience to give us, they often enjoy the company of the very young, for instance grandchildren, and get on extremely well with them. These days there are far more facilities for keeping healthy in the latter years, including special swimming sessions and light aerobics which can all help to make an expanded family life quite as enjoyable as, indeed, many other cultures take as normal. However, planning is what it is all about. If you have made financial provision to meet any expenses which arise because of an elderly relative, it will make those potentially difficult times that much easier to deal with and the situation will be less fraught all round. This book has been about caring for elderly relatives. One day, though, there's every likelihood that it will happen to you.

Appendix: Useful addresses

Abbeyfield Society, 186-192 Darkes Lane, Potters Bar, Hertfordshire EN6 1AB. (0707) 44845.

Age Concern England, Bernard Sunley House, 60 Pitcairn Road, Mitcham, Surrey CR4 3LL. 01-640 5431.

Alzheimer's Disease Society, 158-160 Balham High Road, London SW12 9BN. 01-675 6557.

Association of Crossroads Care Attendant Schemes, 10 Regent Place, Rugby, Warwickshire CV21 2PN. (0788) 73653.

British Nursing Association, 112 Denmark Hill, London SE5 8RX. 01-274 2887.

British Red Cross Society, 9 Grosvenor Crescent, London SW1X 7EJ. 01-235 5454.

Budget BUPA Centre, Gill House, Thames Street, Staines, Middlesex TW18 4SL. (0784) 466188.

BUPA Care for the Elderly, Dolphyn Court, Great Turnstile, Lincoln's Inn Fields, London WC1V 7JU. 01-831 2668.

Carers National Association, First Floor, 21-23 New Road, Chatham, Kent ME4 4QJ. (0634) 813981.

Appendix: Useful addresses

Counsel and Care for the Elderly, Twyman House, 16 Bonny Street, London NW1 9CR. 01-485 1566.

Court of Protection, 24 Kingsway, London WC2B 6HD. 01-405 4300.

The Distressed Gentlefolk's Aid Association, Vicarage Gate House, Vicarage Gate, London W8 4AQ. 01-229 9341.

DSS, Freephone Advice, (0800) 666555.

Elderly Accommodation Counsel, 1 Dunward House, 31 Kensington Court, London W8 5BH. 01-995 8320/01-742 1182.

Help the Aged, 16-18 St James's Walk, London EC1R 0BE. 01-253 0253.

HM Inspector of Anatomy, 160 Great Portland Street, London W1N 5TB. 01-872 9302.

Home Office, E Division, Room 976, 50 Queen Anne's Gate, London SW1 9AT. 01-273 3056.

King's Fund Centre's Informal Caring Support Unit, 126 Albert Street, London NW1 7NF. 01-267 6111.

Legal Aid, Head Office, Newspaper House, 8-16 Great New Street, London EC4A 3BN. 01-353 7411.

Locatex Bureau, PO Box 101, Aberystwyth, Dysed. (0970) 625 626.

Marie Curie Memorial Foundation, 28 Belgrave Square, London SW1X 8QG. 01-235 3325.

National Association of Almshouses, Billingbear Lodge, Wokingham, Berkshire RG11 5RV. (0344) 52922.

Appendix: Useful addresses 119

National Association of Funeral Directors, 618 Warwick Road, Solihull, West Midlands B91 1AA. (021) 711 1343.

National Council for Voluntary Organisations, 26 Bedford Square, London WC1B 3HU, 01-636 4066.

National Housebuilding Council, Buildmark House, Chiltern Avenue, Amersham, Buckinghamshire HP6 5AP, (0494) 434477.

Neighbourhood Energy Action, 214 Bigg Market, Newcastle-upon-Tyne NE1 1UW. (091) 261 5677.

PPP — Beaumont plc, 1 Lonsdale Gardens, Tunbridge Wells, Kent TN1 1NU. (0892) 546655.

Private Patients Plan House, 20 Upperton Road, Eastbourne, East Sussex BN21 1LH. (0323) 410505.

The Treasury Solicitor's Department (BV), Queen Anne's Chambers, 28 Broadway, London SW1H 9JS. 01-210 3000.

War Pensions Branch DSS, Worcross, Blackpool FY5 3TA. (0253) 856123.

Women's Royal Voluntary Service (WRVS) 234-244 Stockwell Road, London SW9 9SP. 01-733 3388.

Other titles in this series

Managing Your Finances	Helen Pridham
Planning Your Pension	Tony Reardon
Buying Your Home	Richard Newell
Your Home in Italy	Flavia Maxwell
Tax for the Self-Employed	David Williams
Your Home in Portugal	Rosemary de Rougemont
Your Home in Spain	Per Svensson
Planning School and College Fees	Danby Block & Amanda Pardoe
Investing in Shares	Hugh Pym & Nick Kochan
Insurance– Are You Covered?	Mihir Bose
Leaving Your Money Wisely	Tony Foreman
Financial Planning for the Over 50s	Robert Leach
Your Home in France	Henry Dyson
Making Your Job Work	David Williams
Tax and Finance for Women	Helen Pridham

Index

Caring at home—
  attendant schemes, care, 57-8
  carers—
    benefits available, 50-1, 57
    generally, 50-1
    practical help, 57
    support, 56-8
  emotional implications—
    decision, help in reaching, 52-3
    generally, 51
    questions relevant, 51-2
  financial implications—
    extra expenses, 53-4
    generally, 53
    working restrictions, 54
  generally, 50
  mental health problems, 57
  physical implications—
    adapting one's own home, 55
    basic nursing, 55
    generally, 54-5
  Rochdale Carer's Charter, 54
  visits at home, health, 57-8
Charities—
  Abbeyfield Society, 72-3, 76-7
  Age Concern, 31-2
  almshouses, 74-5
  Cancer Relief Macmillan Fund, 82
  Centre for Policy on Ageing, 31, 32
  Counsel and Care for Elderly, 61
  Distressed Gentlefolk's Aid
    Association, 73-4
  generally, 31, 32
  Help the Aged, 31, 32
  hospices, 81
  local, 33-4
  major organisations, 31-2
  private home fees, 68
  residential homes, provision, 71
Community charge, 15, 21

Death—
  abroad, 110
  accident, 107
  at home, 106-7
  certificate—
    burial or cremation, 108
    death, 108
    medical, 107
    registration of death, 108
  Coroner's—
    enquiries, 107
    Removal Notice for body, 109
  funeral, *see* Funeral
  generally, 106
  medical aspects, 109
  moving body, 109
  post-mortem, 107
  registrations, 107-8
  transplants, donations for, 109
Disabled persons—
  adaptations to home, 23-4
  attendance allowance, 20
  carers' benefits, 21
  Independent Living Fund, 21
  mobility allowance, 18-19
  premiums, State, 13-14
  Railcard, 30
  rate relief, 21
  travelling, 30
  see also Help at home

Financial planning, 114-16
Fuel costs—
  assistance, 27
  meters, 27-8
  social fund payment, 17, 27
Funeral—
  arrangements—
    choice, 110-11
    estimates, 111

Funeral—*continued*
  pre-paid, 111
  wishes of deceased, 111
  burial, 112
  Code of Conduct, 110, 111
  costs—
    advance from estate, 113
    authority's payment, 113
    employees, 113
    payment, 112
    social fund payments, 17, 112–13
    war pensioner, 113
  cremation, 111–12

Health costs—
  abroad, 29–30
  dental care, 28
  generally, 28
  hearing aids, 29
  insurance, 28, 30, 77–80
  opticians, 29
  prescriptions, 29
  private care, 28
Help at home—
  adaptations, 23–4
  finance, 24–7
  availability, 22–3
  caring at one's own home, *see*
    Caring at home generally, 22–3
  overcoming disabilities, 23–4
  see also Fuel costs *and* Health costs
Home—
  adaptability—
    builders, reputable, 40
    finance, *see* finance for adaptions
    generally, 39
    obtaining advice, 39–40
    one's own home, 55
  buying—
    discount schemes, 45–6
    leasehold schemes, 44
    licence schemes, 45
    limited capital, 43–6
    loan-stock schemes, 45
    right to buy scheme, 43
    shared ownership, 44–5
  capital release, 91, 95
  choice, 35–6
  draughtproofing, funding fitting, 26–7
  finance for adaptations—
    generally, 24

Home—*continued*
  grants—
    council, 26–7
    home improvement, 25
    intermediate, 25
    repairs, 25
  loans—
    conventional, 25–6
    interest only, 26
    maturity, 26
  generally, 35
  granny flats, 46
  help at, *see* Help at home
  Income Plans, 91–2
    tax, 92–3
  Inheritance Tax, 93
  insulation, funding fitting, 26–7
  investment bond income schemes, 95
  loans, interest only, 95
  location, 36–37
  maintenance cost—
    council properties, 41
    generally, 40–1
    housing association properties, 41
    responsibilities—
      landlords', 41
      tenants', 41
  mortgage annuity, 91–2
    tax, 92–3
  moving—
    council tenants, 42–3
    housing association tenants, 42, 43
    National Mobility Scheme, 42
    schemes, 42–3
    Tenants' Exchange Scheme, 42–3
  Reversion Schemes, 93–4
  security—
    alarm systems—
      funding fitting, 26, 38
      generally, 38
    generally, 37–8, 38–9
  sheltered housing—
    code of conduct, 49
    council provision, 47
    facilities, 48
    generally, 46–7, 48–9
    private sector, 47
    selling, 48
    services, 48
  survey, 41
  telephone, 38
Hospices, 80–1

Index

Inheritance Tax—
  charge, 101-2
  Home Income Plan, 93
  imposition, 101
  reduction, 93, 102-3

Legal aspects—
  costs—
    assistance, 30
    Citizens Advice Bureau, 30
  Court of Protection—
    application to, 90
    purpose, 89-90
    receiver, 90
    visitor from, 90
  financial matters—
    agents, 87
    appointees, 87-8
    generally, 86-87
  generally, 83
  guardianship, 83-4
  medical treatment, 85-6
  placement in residential care, 84
  powers of attorney, 88-9
  treatment of elderly, 84-5
  trusts, 89
  Wills, *see* Wills
Lifeline system, 32
Local authorities—
  home, help at, *see* Help at Home

Medical care—
  consent to treatment, 84-5, 85-6
  assumption, 86
  generally, 76
  NHS waiting lists, 77-8
  private health insurance schemes—
    Budget BUPA Scheme, 79
    exclusions, 79
    Family Health Plan, PPP's, 78-9
    generally, 77-8
    premium rates, 79-80
    provision under, 79
    Retirement Health Policy, PPP's, 78-9
    tax relief, 78
  refusal of treatment, 84-5
  terminally ill—
    home units, 81-2
    hospices, 80-1
  see also Health costs *and* Nursing care

Nursing care—
  centres for, 77
  nursing homes, *see* Residential care, nursing homes
  private, in home, 80
  Private Patient's Plan (PPP), 77
  see also Health costs *and* Medical care

Pensions—
  private schemes—
    additional voluntary contributions, 97-8
    free-standing, 97
    generally, 3, 96-7
    occupational schemes, 97-8
    opting out, 99
    personal, 98-9
  State—
    basic, 6
    change in retired population, 2
    claiming from—
      abroad, 10
      hospital, 10-11
    deferring retirement, 7
    divorced claimants, 9
    earnings—
      related scheme, 7-8
      rule, 6
    generally, 5
    graduated, 6-7
    Home Responsibilities Protection scheme, 8
    inadequacy, 3
    increasing, 7
    married women, 6
    non-contributory, 8
    over 80s, 8
    separated claimants, 10
    SERPS, 7-8
Poll tax, 15, 21
Population—
  ageing, 2
  average age, 1-2
  control of growth, 1, 2
  life expectancy, 1

Residential care—
  choice of home—
    Counsel and Care for Elderly, 61
    Elderly Accommodation Counsel, 60-1

Residential care—*continued*
  Grace Link, 60
  making, 60
  types, 61
  Community Care Report, 70
  generally, 59-60
  homes—
    authorisation, 62
    code of practice, Home Life, 62, 87, 88
    generally, 61-2
    inspection, 62
    registration, 62
  local authority homes—
    availability of place, 63
    Community Care Report, 70
    inspection, 63
    payment, 64
    provision, 62-3
    trial stay, 63
  nursing homes—
    BUPA, 77
    care provided, 76-7
    meaning, 68
    NHS scheme, 69, 76
      payment, 69-70
      assistance, 69-70
    registration, 68
    requirements, 68
  private homes—
    charges, 66
    assistance, 66-8
    organisations for, 65
    payment, 66-8
    provision, 64-5
    registration, 65
    suitability, 66
  voluntary homes—
    Abbeyfield homes, 72-3, 76-7
    almshouses, 74-5
    availability, 71-2
    Distressed Gentlefolk's Aid Association, 73-4
    generally, 71-2, 75
Retirement—
  planning, 114, 116

State—
  attendance allowance, 20

State—*continued*
  carers' benefits, 21
  crisis loan, 16-17
  extra allowances—
    Christmas bonus, 15
    home owners, 15
    housing benefit, 15-16
    social fund, 16-17
  home, help at, *see* Help at home
  income support—
    case studies, 14
    disability premiums, 13-14
    generally, 11, 12
    meaning of income, 12
    premiums, additional, 13-14
    savings rule, 11-12
  invalidity benefit, 19
  mobility allowance, 18-19
  pensions, *see* Pensions, State

Travelling—
  car-sharing schemes, 33
  discounted fares, 30
  minibuses, 32, 33

Widows—
  children, allowance, 8
  payment, 8
  pension, 8-9
Wills—
  Deeds of Variation, 104-5
  Inheritance Tax, *see* Inheritance Tax
  intestacy—
    administrator, acting as, 104
    generally, 103
    no relatives, 104
    no surviving partner, 103-4
    surviving partner—
      with children, 103
      without children, 103
  living Will, 85
  making, 100
  need for, 100
  personal representative, acting as, 104
  probate, 104